American Data

from the

Aberdeen Journal

1748–1783

by

David Dobson

CLEARFIELD

Printed for
Clearfield Company, Inc. by
Genealogical Publishing Co., Inc.
Baltimore, Maryland
1998

Reprinted for
Clearfield Company, Inc. by
Genealogical Publishing Co., Inc.
Baltimore, Maryland
2004

International Standard Book Number: 0-8063-4766-X

Made in the United States of America

INTRODUCTION

Newspapers represent one of the potentially most fruitful sources for genealogical and historical research, yet they remain generally underutilized.

Scottish newspapers are no exception. There exist 350 years' worth of newspapers in the National Library of Scotland and, to a lesser extent, in libraries and archives throughout the land that await scrutiny by researchers. The earliest example dates from 1641 and is a reprint of the *London Diurnal Occurances*. The earliest surviving Scots newspaper is the *Mercurius Scoticus* of 26 August 1651. Apart from that there are examples of eleven different newspapers of the seventeenth century and thirty-two of the eighteenth century. Initially, Edinburgh had the virtual monopoly, but this was broken by the *Glasgow Journal* of 1741 and the *Aberdeen Journal* of 1748.

The *Aberdeen Journal* is one of Scotland's oldest continuous newspapers. Founded in December of 1747 as the *Aberdeen Journal*, it remained under that title until it merged with the *Aberdeen Free Press* in 1922; it stayed the *Aberdeen Press and Journal* until 1939 when it was retitled the *Press and Journal*. The columns of the *Aberdeen Journal* contain many references to colonial America between 1748 and 1783 that have been extracted to form this work. Only the material that originated in Scottish sources has been selected, and data culled from English or colonial newspapers have not been included. The period covered includes the third quarter of the eighteenth century when the Chesapeake tobacco trade was under the control of Glasgow merchants and Scottish emigration was becoming significant. Some of the material is unique—there are references to emigration, felons being banished to the plantations, shipping links that facilitated emigration, advertisements for indentured servants, news of events in the colonies, details on Scots regiments fighting in the French and Indian Wars and the Revolution, reports of privateers, letters from America, and obituaries of local emigrants there. It therefore provides a fascinating insight into social and economic links between colonial America and Scotland, particularly Aberdeen.

David Dobson
St. Andrews, Scotland

#4   "Advertisement. That James Gray, merchant in Aberdeen, will set out for Virginia betwixt and the 20th February next. This is therefore advertising all kinds of tradesmen and others that by applying to the said James Gray they who have a mind to go abroad for a few years will meet with better encouragement than has been formerly given. N B A proper person either in town or country that will be at the trouble to engage servants, by applying to the said James Gray will be handsomely rewarded." 19.1.1748.

#15   "Glasgow. Eliza, Blair, from Virginia being much damaged on her passage home bore away for Antigua and was taken by a Spanish privateer and carried to Hispaniola from whence the crew was exchanged and brought to Jamaica by a cartel ship." 5.4.1748.

#17   Nancy, Master James Park, sailed from Aberdeen via Norway and Ireland to Maryland, 22.4.1748.

Anna of Aberdeen, master James Ferguson, from Montrose via Aberdeen to Virginia, 4.1748.

#20   Glasgow. Rae, a galley, bound for Virginia ran aground on a sandbank 8 leagues off that coast. 17.5.1748.

#24   Extract of a letter from Crail 3.6.1748, re the Friendship of London, Captain William Clelland, with another merchant ship, having taken the north passage from Charleston, South Carolina, for London, was attacked by a French privateer off Rona, 10.5.1748.

#25   Greenock 11.6.1748, Mayflower, galliot, ...; Prince William, Wardrope; Anderson, Campbell; Jenny, Paterson; Matty, Gray; and Jenny, Cunningham, arrived with tobacco from Virginia. Betty of Liverpool arrived in Greenock from Philadelphia. 21.7.1748.

#25   Leithly, master John Lickly, from Aberdeen to Virginia 7.1748

#31   Glasgow. Mayflower, Steil, and John and Anne, master ... Service, both of and from Irvine to Barbados, were taken by a French privateer and carried to Bayonne. 2.4.1748.

Ruby, Gordon, from Aberdeen to Virginia 2.4.1748.

#36   Extract from a letter on board Little Mally of Glasgow, 17.4.1748, 100 leagues east of the Capes of Virginia re the Betty, pink, of Glasgow, master James Aitken, which had been taken by a Spanish privateer off Virginia but had subsequently escaped. 6.9.1748.

#39	Extract of a letter from Virginia, dated Norfolk 21.7.1748, re the activities of Spanish privateers of the coast of Virginia, and Betty of Glasgow which had been taken by the Spanish but through damage had put into New York where the ship and crew were liberated. 9.1748.
#40	Greenock, 24.9.1748. Amity of Glasgow to sail from Port Glasgow to Jamaica with passengers 1 11.1748.
#41	James Young, tenant in Home, guilty of fire raising, was banished to the Plantations in America for life, at Jedburgh 20.10.1748.
#42	"Advertisement. That betwixt and 1 February next there is a good ship to sail from Aberdeen to Antigua. These are therefore to certify all good tradesmen, those who can write and keep accompts, men skilled in distempers of black cattle and horses, and other servants from 12 years old and upwards. That open apply to John Elphinstone or Andrew Garioch, merchants in Aberdeen, they will be indented for 4 years only, find great encouragement than ever given from this place and will be strongly recommended by the said Andrew Garioch who left that island not 15 months ago. Further particulars refers to an advertisement placed the 10th current." 15.11.1748.
#48	Arrived in Greenock 20.11.1748 - Free Mason Paterson, from Virginia with tobacco, Adventure Pollock, from Jamaica with sugar; sailed - Argyll, Montgomerie, to Cork and Antigua, Glencairn to St Kitts, and Amity, Aitken, to Jamaica.
#49	Greenock, 26.11.1748. Thetis, Andrew, and Prosperity, Boyd, arrived from Virginia with tobacco.
#50	Greenock, 31.12.1748. Archibald, Watson, to Barbados, and Montgomerie, Dunlop, to Virginia.
#54	"Advertisement. That the good ship The Mary and Betty, James Melven master, 140 ton burthen, will sail from Aberdeen to the fruitful island of Antigua betwixt and the 1st February next. Therefore all men servants of 12 years and upwards upon application to John Elphinston or Andrew Garioch, merchants in Aberdeen, will be indented only for 4 years and get greater encouragement than ever given from this place. Tradesmen there that can write and keep accompts

and men skilled in distemper of black cattle and horses will get from £15 to £10 per annum during the years of their indenture. And all servants get at least £50 after the expiration of their time and they will be received by the said Andrew Garioch who left that island 18 months ago. N.B. there is good accommodation for passengers." 17.1.1749.

#55   Greenock, 7.1.1749. Neptune, Weir, Peggie, Walkingshaw, and Elizabeth, Morrison, arrived from Virginia with tobacco.
Advert as above for Antigua, plus "N.B. Andrew Garioch will be at Mr Scot's at Inveruray, Monday 23rd current, at Kinethmont the 24th, Miln of North 25th, Mr Mellis's in Huntly the 26th, and at Mr Gillespie's in Old Meldrum on Saturday 25th, so that he can be spoke with at either of these places by servants who incline to indent for Antigua." 17.1.1749.
"Greenock of Inverkeithing, Roxburgh, from Maryland with 170 hogsheads of tobacco was put ashore at Cairnbulg last week." 17.1.1749.

#59   Greenock, 4.2.1749. Duke of Cumberland, Brown, arrived from Virginia with tobacco.

#60   Greenock, 11.2.1749. Mary, Dundas, arrived from Maryland with tobacco. Charming Lilly, Cunningham, to Virginia with bale goods.

#61   Anderson, Campbell, arrived in Loch Ryan from Virginia 3.1749.

#63   Ann of Aberdeen, Arbuthnot lately Ferguson, arrived in Aberdeen from Virginia, 21.3.1749.

#64   Aberdeen. Betty and Mary, Melven, sailed to Antigua, and Diligence, Duncan, to Virginia, 21.3.1749.

#66   Greenock, 25.3.1749. Betty, Jeffrey, arrived from Virginia with tobacco. Britannia, Shaw, to Virginia with bale goods.

#67   Greenock, 1.4.1749. Mary, Dundas, Prince William, Smith, Duke of Cumberland, Brown, and Thetis, Andrew, to Virginia with bale goods.
Aberdeen. Leathly, Lickly, arrived from Virginia with tobacco, 4.1749.

#68   Greenock, 8.4.1749. Elizabeth, Morrison, to Maryland with bale goods, and Jean, Barbour, to Barbados with herring.

#69	Queensferry of Dumfries, arrived in Virginia from Morlais 4.1749.
#70	Extract from a letter from Richmond, Virginia, praising the quality of linen sent there by the British Linen Company of Edinburgh, 7.2.1749.

Advertisement. "That any young man bred as a tailor who is good at his business and can cut and shape well who will engage for 3 or 4 years and go over to Virginia, let them apply to John Elphinstone, merchant in Aberdeen, who will enter into an indenture with them and oblige himself to pay them £10 Sterling yearly with bed, board and washing. And in case they don't like the country when there, he shall oblige himself to bring them back to Aberdeen on his own charge. If there is any other tradesmen such as smiths, wrights, bricklayers, etc has a mind to engage let them apply as above and he will give them very great encouragement, and dare venture to say that scarce a tradesman in this country that can make near so much free money yearly with his own hand." 2.5.1749.

Ruby of Aberdeen, Gordon, arrived in Aberdeen from Virginia in 25 days. 5.1749.

#71	Greenock, 29.4.1749. Diligence, Dunlop, to Maryland with bale goods.
#72	Greenock, 8.5.1749. Betty, Scott, and James, Shannon, arrived from Virginia with tobacco.
#73	Anne of Aberdeen, Thomson, and Dispatch, Thistlewait, from Aberdeen to Virginia 5.1749.
#74	"On Thursday James Coutts, Arthur Gibbons, Isobel Ogilvie and Margaret Pirie, who were banished, were put upon a vessel in the harbor for Virginia." 30.5.1749.
#75	Greenock, 27 5.1749 Pearl, Francis, arrived from Virginia with tobacco.

Edinburgh. Industry of Leith, Andrew Cowan, arrived in Charleston, South Carolina, 31.3.1749.

#76	Alexander and Ann, Clark, from Aberdeen to Virginia 6.1749.
#78	Greenock, 6.1749. Jeannie, Douglas, and Dunlop, Alexander, arrived in Greenock from Virginia.
#80	Leathly, Lickly, from Aberdeen to Virginia 7.1749.
#82	Thomas Bradshaw, a former soldier, ... Long, and ... Hall, were sent from Edinburgh under guard to Glasgow for shipment to the Plantations never to return, 18.7.1749.

St Andrew of Glasgow, Blair, at Peterhead from Maryland with tobacco 7.1749.

#83   Prince William, Smith, arrived in Virginia 18.5.1749 from the Clyde.

St Andrew of Glasgow, Blair, arrived in Aberdeen from Virginia with tobacco 8.1749.

#85   Adventure, Smith, from Glasgow to Jamaica with felons; Donald, Andrew, Jenny, Cunningham. and Susannah, Steil, arrived in Greenock from Virginia with tobacco, 5.8.1749; Dunlop, Alexander, from Greenock to Virginia, and _ Endeavour, Smith, from Greenock to Jamaica, both with bale goods, 5.8.1749.

#86   Nelly, Galbraith, arrived in Greenock from Virginia with tobacco 12.8.1749, Kingston, Chisholm, arrived in Greenock from St Kitts with sugar 12.8.1749.

John Smith, sentenced to death for counterfeiting, agreed instead to transport himself to HM Plantations never to return, Edinburgh 14.8.1749.

#88   Pearl, Francis, and Jeanie, Douglas, from Greenock to Virginia with bale goods 29.8.1749; Mattie, Gray, arrived in Greenock from Virginia with tobacco 26.8.1749.

Montgomerie, Dunlop, and Thetis, Andrew, arrived in Fairlie Roads from Virginia 8.1749.

#89   Glasgow 4.9.1749. Grizell, Hamilton, arrived in Lamlash from Virginia; Montgomerie, Dunlop, and Boyd, Campbell, arrived in Greenock with tobacco 2.9.1749; Grand Turk, Kerr, arrived in Greenock from Barbados with sugar, and Prosperity, McCunn, arrived in Greenock from Boston with lumber and oil; Menie, Stewart, to Philadelphia from Greenock with bale goods.

#90   Glasgow 17.8.1749. Jane, Glen, arrived at Barbados from Greenock, and Bell, arrived in Saltcoats from Virginia Greenock, 9.9.1749. Grizel, Hamilton, and Duke of Cumberland, Brown, arrived with tobacco, and Dove, Sempill, arrived from Jamaica with sugar.

#91   St Andrew, master ... Gordon, was loading goods in Aberdeen for Virginia, 26.9.1749.

#92   Greenock, 23.9.1749. Amity, Aitken, arrived from Jamaica with sugar, and Montrose, Graham, sailed to Antigua with bale goods.

#92   Edinburgh, 3.10.1749. "By a gentleman lately come from Nova Scotia we are informed that there are upwards of

12,000 people besides 2 regiments of HM forces
already settled in that colony and that they are very busy
clearing ground for building houses, sowing corn, etc."

#93 Betty and Mary, Melvin, arrived in Aberdeen from Antigua
10.1749.

#94 Greenock, 7.10.1749. Mary, Dundas, arrived from Maryland
with tobacco.

#95 St Andrew, Gordon, from Aberdeen to Virginia 17.10.1749.

William Hamilton yr., Upper Craiginputtock, was banished for
7 years for assault, at Dumfries 20.10.1749.

"Last Thursday John Watson and Christian Ironside were put
on a ship for transportation according to their sentences,
as was Ann Watt who was brought from Forfar"
Aberdeen 24.10.1749.

#96 Greenock, 21.10.1749. The Bogle, Fleming, and The
Friendship, Colquhoun, arrived from Virginia with
tobacco, while The Prosperity, McCunn, and The James
and John, Purdie, sailed to Boston with bale goods.

#97 Tryton, Boyd, and The William, Simpson, arrived in Glasgow
from Virginia 11.1749.

Greenock, 28.10.1749 The Cochran, Steil, The Dorothy,
Shannon, and The Mary, Main, arrived from Virginia with
tobacco.

Jedburgh, 21.10.1749. John Young, late soldier in Colonel
Fraser's Regiment of Marines, and Margaret Young his
wife, guilty of theft and felony, were banished to
America.

#98 Greenock, 4.11.1749. The Duke, Jamieson, The Clyde,
Boyd, and The Anderson, Campbell, arrived from
Virginia with tobacco.

Diligence of Aberdeen, Duncan, arrived in Aberdeen from
Maryland with tobacco 11.1749.

Leathly, Lickly, and Anne, Thomson, arrived in Virginia
from Aberdeen.

#99 Greenock, 11.11.1749. The Charming Lilly, Cunningham,
arrived from Virginia with tobacco. Peggy of Dumfries,
Blair, arrived in Kirkcudbright from Virginia with tobacco
3.11.1749.

#100 Greenock, 18.11.1749. Nancy, Robertson, arrived from
Virginia with tobacco.

#101 George, Crawford, arrived in Greenock from Virginia with
tobacco.

Extract of a letter from the James River, Virginia, dated 25.8.1749 praising the quality of Scots linen.

Donald Fraser sr., thief, and Jean McPherson, guilty of childmurder, were brought under guard to Aberdeen to be taken from there to Glasgow or Edinburgh for transportation to the Plantations.

#103 Neptune, Weir, arrived in Greenock from Virginia 12.1749 with reports of damage to property and shipping in Virginia between 28th and 30th October due to a hurricane - Albany, Brown, was lost off Cape Henry, Free Mason, Paterson, was 'bulg'd' in Linhaven Bay, Graeme, Hunter, ashore in Linhaven Bay, Bess, Heasty, James, Shannon, and The Britannia, Wallace, were driven ashore in the Elizabeth River, while damage occurred to tobacco stored in warehouses.

Pearl, Francis, arrived in Virginia from the Clyde; Christian was at Philadelphia from the Clyde; while Edinburgh, Lyon, arrived at Spithead from Carolina.

Advertisement. "That betwixt and 1st February next there is a good ship to sail from Aberdeen to Antigua. Therefore all men servants, from 12 years old and upwards, will be indentured only for 4 years and receive good usage in all respects upon their application to Alexander Livingston, John Elphinston, Andrew Burnet and Andrew Garioch, merchants in Aberdeen, or James Winchester, merchant in Fraserburgh. For further particulars refers to advertisements published 28th instant and to James Winchester who recently arrived from that island. N.B. No persons of bad character to be received." 19.12.1749.

#104 Grizel, Hamilton, from Greenock to Virginia with bale goods and Amity, Aitken, and Cassandra, McMillan, from Greenock to Jamaica, with bale goods, 12.1749. Adventure, Smith, arrived in Kingston, Jamaica, 28.9.1749. Donald, Andrew, arrived in Virginia from the Clyde while Bowling, Campbell arrived in Virginia from Piscataway.

#105 Edinburgh, Ninian Bruce, arrived in Burntisland from Jamaica 28.12.1749.

#106 John and Robert, Craig, arrived in Glasgow from Virginia with lumber.

7

Alexander McDonald, reprieved on condition of self transportation to HM Plantations in America, at Edinburgh 12.1749.

#107 Archibald, Watson, arrived in Barbados from Greenock. Greenock, 6.1.1750. Dunbarton, Watson, and Thistle, Coulter, arrived from Virginia with tobacco. Grand Turk, Wyllie, to Barbados with herring. Alexander Livingstone to be transported to HM Plantations in America never to return, Edinburgh, 1.1750.

#108 Greenock, 13.1.1750. St Paul, A. Mason, arrived from Virginia with tar and turpentine. Thomas Webster, servant to Colonel Price, died in Jamaica 6.1749. He left a legacy which was to be claimed from David Verner, Professor of Philosophy at Marischal College. Dispatch bound from Virginia to Aberdeen was at Plymouth.

#111 Anne of Aberdeen, Thomson, arrived in Aberdeen from Virginia with tobacco.

#112 Greenock, 10.2.1750. Britannia, Wallace, Elizabeth, Morrison, and Buchanan, Orr, arrived from Virginia with tobacco. Dispatch of Newcastle, Thistlewaite, arrived in Aberdeen from Virginia with tobacco, 2.1750.

#113 Betty and Mary of Aberdeen, Gelly, from Aberdeen to Antigua 2.1750.

#117 Grizel, Hamilton, arrived in Virginia from the Clyde. Bess, Dick, arrived in Greenock from Virginia with lumber 17.3.1750, and Newal, Smith, arrived in Greenock from Maryland 26.3.1750.

#118 Robert, Orr, arrived in Greenock from Virginia with tar and tobacco 24.3.1750, and Greenock, McCunn, arrived in Greenock from Virginia with tobacco 24.3.1750. Eglinton, McAuslane, from Greenock to South Carolina with herring, 3.1750. Duke, Jamieson, Thistle, Boyd, and Nelly, Galbraith, from Greenock to Virginia with bale goods, 3.1750. Anne of Aberdeen, Thomson, from Aberdeen to Virginia.

#119 Greenock, 31.3.1750. Mary, Dundas, Boyd, Campbell, Boyd, Campbell, Friendship, Paterson, Diligence, Dunlop, and Duke of Cumberland, Brown, to Virginia with bale goods. Miriam, Thomson, to Jamaica with herring and Kingston, Chisholm, to St Kitts with bale goods.

#120 Greenock, 7.4.1750. Catherine, Steil, to Virginia with bale goods.
Ruby of Aberdeen, Gordon, from Aberdeen to Virginia with Aberdeen-made Osnaburgs, 4.1750.
#121 Greenock, 14.4.1750. Bogle, Fleming, Cochrane, Steil, and Mary, Jaffrie, to Virginia with bale goods.
#122 Adventure, Smith, arrived in Greenock from Jamaica with sugar and rum, 21.4.1750, while Pelham, Youle, sailed to Virginia with bale goods.
"This gives notice to all masons, wrights and farmers or those bred in the farming way, who are willing to go to the rich, pleasant and wholesome island of St Christophers that they may apply to William Ogilvie, merchant in Banff, who will not only give them free passage but will give them handsome encouragement for 4 or 5 years service, after which they are free." 4.1750.
#123 Greenock, 28.4.1750. Jane and Mary, Rogers, arrived from Virginia with tobacco, and Ann, Young, sailed to Boston with bale goods.
Hugh Simpson, sheep stealer, sentenced to be transported, at Dumfries 5.1750.
#126 Greenock, 19.5.1750. Greenock, McCumm, to Boston with bale goods.
St Andrew of Aberdeen, Gordon, arrived in Virginia.
#127 Greenock, 26.5.1750. Graeme, Hunter, Pearl, Francis, Scot, Ewing, and Jenny, Douglas, arrived from Virginia with tobacco, while Murdoch, Hamilton sailed to Virginia with bale goods.
Elizabeth McKenzie, a fire raiser, was banished to the Plantations, at Inverness 19.3.1750.
#128 Houston, Douglas, arrived in Greenock from St Kitts 11 6 1750
Greenock, 2.6.1750. Mary, Scot, James, Shannon, and Donald, Andrew, arrived from Virginia with tobacco.
#129 Glencairn, Cassandra, and Amity, arrived in St Kitts and Antigua.
Greenock, 9.6.1750. Dunlop, Alexander, arrived from Virginia with tobacco.
Grizel, Hamilton, arrived from Virginia 16.6.1750.
#131 Greenock, 30.6.1750. Annabella, Knox, to Virginia with bale goods.
#132 Jean and Mary, Roger, to Virginia with bale goods.

9

Alexander and Anne of Aberdeen, Clark, arrived in Aberdeen
from Virginia with tobacco.

#133   Greenock, 7.7.1750. President, Dunlop, arrived from Virginia
with tobacco, while Argyll, Montgomerie, arrived from
St Kitts with sugar.

"For Virginia. About the first of August next Jane and
Elizabeth of Aberdeen, Thomas Smith commander. If
any men or women servants or mechanicks incline to go
thither they may apply to John Leslie, merchant in
Aberdeen, or Alexander Annand, merchant in Old
Aberdeen, who will agree with them on the best terms."
17.7.1750.

#134   Kingston, Chisholm, arrived in St Kitts.

#135   Jeannie, Somerville, and Mary, Jaffrey, arrived in Virginia.

Alexander Stewart and John Campbell, shopbreakers, were
banished to HM Plantations in America, at Edinburgh
2.7.1750.

#136   Bogle, Fleming, arrived in Virginia.

Greenock 28.7.1750. Thetis, Andrew, arrived from Virginia
with tobacco, while James, Campbell, sailed to Virginia
with bale goods.

#137   Leith Galley, Thomson, arrived in Jamaica from Leith, while
Friendship, Paterson, and Mary, Dundas, arrived in
Virginia.

Greenock 4.8.1750. Prince Charles, Edgar, arrived from
Jamaica with sugar and rum, while Dreghorn, Andrew,
and Pearl, Jeffrey, sailed to Virginia with bale goods.

Alexander and Anne of Aberdeen, sailed from Aberdeen to
Ireland and Virginia, while Jean and Elizabeth of
Aberdeen sailed to Virginia.

#138   Nelly, Galbreath, arrived in Greenock from Virginia with
tobacco 11 8 1750

Greenock 11.8.1750. Cassandra, McMillan, arrived from
Jamaica with sugar, while Nancy, McLeish, sailed to
Virginia with bale goods.

Alexander and Elizabeth of Aberdeen, Smith, from Aberdeen
to Maryland.

#139   Alexander and Ann of Aberdeen, Clark, from Aberdeen to
Virginia 8.1750.

#140   Greenock, 25.8.1750. Grand Turk, Wyllie, arrived from
Barbados with wine, and Kingston, Chisholm, arrived
from St Kitts with sugar.

Leathly of Aberdeen, Lickly, arrived in Aberdeen from
    Maryland with tobacco. Ruby of Aberdeen, Scott,
    arrived in Virginia.

#141   Greenock 1.9.1750. Amity, Aitken, arrived fron Jamaica with
    rum and sugar, while Grizel, Johnston sailed to Virginia,
    and Betty, Warden, sailed to Maryland, both with bale
    goods.

#142   Diligence, Dunlop, arrived in Campbelltown from Virginia
    9.1750. Friendship, Paterson, arrived in Greenock from
    Virginia 9.9.1750.

Greenock, 8.9.1750. Hawk, McCunn, to Boston with bale
    goods.

Elizabeth Dunbar, Banff, guilty of child murder was banished
    to the Plantations for life, at Aberdeen 9.1750.

#143   Matty, Gray, arrived in Greenock from Virginia 16.9.1750.

Greenock, 15.9.1750. Diligence, Dunlop, arrived from
    Virginia with tobacco and Montrose, Graham, arrived
    from Antigua with sugar.

#144   Thistle, Coulter, and Adventure, Mein, arrived in Virginia
    from the Clyde.

Greenock, 22.9.1750. Mary, Jaffray,Mary, Dundas, and
    Peggie, Montgomerie, arrived from Virginia with
    tobacco, while Glencairn, Glasgow, arrived from Antigua
    with sugar.

#145   Greenock, 29.9.1750. Cassandra, Hutchison, left for Jamaica
    via Cork, and Argyll, Montgomerie, left for Antigua via
    Cork, both with bale goods.

#148   Industry of Leith, master Andrew Cowan, at Lisbon on way to
    Carolina 10.1750.

#149   Greenock, 27.10.1750. William, McLean, to Virginia with bale
    goods.

#150   Ann of Aberdeen, Thomson, arrived in Aberdeen from
    Virginia, 11.1750.

#151   Robert arrived in the Clyde from St Kitts and Christian
    arrived in the Clyde from Virginia, 11.1750.

Annabella, Knox, Neptune, West, and Buchanan, Orr,
    arrived in Virginia from the Clyde.

Peter Taylor, who had been sentenced to death at Perth, was
    pardoned on the condition he was transported to the
    Plantations for life, 11.1750.

Ruby of Aberdeen, Gordon, arrived in Aberdeen with tobacco
    from Virginia 11.1750.

#152	Greenock 17.11.1750. Hopton, Steil, arrived from Boston in ballast; Robert, Shannon, arrived from St Kitts with sugar; and Christian, Brodie, and Cochrane, Steil, both arrived from Virginia with tobacco.
	William Martin to be transported to the Plantations, 11.1750.
	St Andrew of Aberdeen, Gordon, arrived in Aberdeen from Virginia, with tobacco 11 1750
#154	Thistle, John Boyd, arrived in Leith from Virginia with 400 hogsheads of tobacco, 12.1750.
	Greenock, 1.12.1750. Greenock, McCunn, Joanna, Semple, and Adventure, Mein, arrived from Virginia with tobacco. Montrose, Graham, to Antigua with bale goods.
	Betty and Mary of Aberdeen, master Lewis Gelly, from Antigua to Aberdeen, wrecked off Isle of Lewis 16.11.1750.
#155	Jean, Somerville, and Boyd, Campbell, arrived in Lamlash from Virginia 12.1750; Jean and Mary, Rodger, and Pearl, arrived in Virginia from the Clyde, while Hawk, McCunn, arrived in Boston from the Clyde.
	Greenock, 8.12.1750. Duke, Jamieson, Bogle, Fleming, Dreghorn, Andrew, and Charming Lilly, King, arrived from Virginia with tobacco, while Boston Packet, McCall, arrived from Boston with lumber.
#156	Amity of Ayr arrived at Lamlash from Virginia.
#157	Lilly of Dumfries, Blair, arrived in Dumfries from Virginia with tobacco, 12.1750; Murdoch, Hamilton, arrived in Greenock from Virginia with tobacco, 22.12.1750.
	George Young, a tinker, guilty of assault at Muir of Kinnellar, was banished to America for life, at Aberdeen 1.1751.
#158	Greenock, 29.12.1750 Anderson, Campbell, arrived from Virginia with tobacco; Mary, McMillan, to Jamaica and Robert, Shannon, to Cork and St Kitts both with herring.
#159	Annabella, Knox, Jean and Mary, Rodger, Jenny, Montgomerie, Duke of Cumberland, Brown, and Jenny, Cunningham, arrived in Greenock from Virginia with tobacco 5.1.1751.
#160	William Sharp, William Paterson, William Clark and John Clark, rioters in Alloa, banished to the Plantations for 7 years, at Edinburgh 1.1751.
#162	"For Antigua. Against the 15th of this current month the ship

Planter, Captain James Elphinstone commander. Any who have a mind to go. Passengers with the said vessel may apply to John Elphinstone, merchant in Aberdeen, or to Captain Elphinstone who will be found in the house of the said John Elphinstone. N.B. She is a fine new vessel and has good accommodation." 5 2.1751

#163   Edinburgh, Lyon, sailed from Greenock to South Carolina with bale goods 2.2.1751; Planter, Elphinstone, arrived in Aberdeen from Montrose bound for Antigua.

#164   Kingston, Chisholm, sailed from Greenock to St Kitts with bale goods and herring 9.2.1751.

#165   Greenock, 16.2.1751. Donald, Andrew, arrived from Virginia with tobacco, and Greenock, McCunn, sailed for Virginia with bale goods.

#166   Ruby of Aberdeen, Gordon, Adventure of Aberdeen, Melvin, and St Andrew of Aberdeen, Cooper, sailed from Aberdeen to Virginia, while Leathly of Aberdeen, Lickly, sailed from Aberdeen to Maryland, 3.1751.

#167   Rose, Yuill, Hawk, Campbell, and Glasgow, McCunn, arrived in Greenock from Boston with timber, tar and oil, Grizel, Johnston, and Bell, Ramsay, arrived from Virginia with tobacco, and Miriam, Tomlinson, sailed to Jamaica with herring, 4.3.1751; Jean and Elizabeth of Aberdeen, Smith, arrived in Aberdeen in 39 days from the Capes of Virginia, with tobacco, 5.1751.

#169   St Andrew of Aberdeen, Cooper, and Adventure of Aberdeen, Melvin, from Aberdeen to Virginia, while Leathly of Aberdeen, Lickly, from Aberdeen to Maryland, 3.1751.

#170   Boston Packet, Laing, and Amity, sailed to Boston, while Binning, Steil, and Nelly, Galbraith, sailed to Virginia with bale goods from Greenock 23 3 1751.

"Last week James Young, William Martin, Elizabeth Dunbar and Betty Grant were put on a vessel bound for Virginia in order to their transportation to the West Indies." Aberdeen, 2.4.1751.

#171   Dorothy of Glasgow arrived in Cadiz from Virginia.

Nancy, McLeish, and Graemie, Hunter, arrived in Greenock from Virginia with tobacco 30.3.1751.

#174   Dreghorn, Andrew, and Hawk, Heastie, sailed from Greenock to Virginia with bale goods, 13.4.1751.

#175	Greenock, 27.4.1751. Dutchess, Young, arrived from Boston with oak and timber, while Duke of Cumberland, Dunlop, Donald, Andrew, and Jean and Mary, Rodger, sailed to Virginia with bale goods. William Thomson, Cromarty, a thief, was banished and to be transported, at Inverness 4.1751. Alexander MacKenzie and his wife Mary Dyer, gypsies, guilty of theft, banished to America, in Dumfries 25.5.1751. John McIntosh or Grant, a thief, and Elizabeth Cruickshank, a child murderer, were banished to the Plantations, in Aberdeen 5.1751. Laetitia, Wall, arrived in Aberdeen from Virginia with tobacco 5.1751.
#177	Jean, Motherhill, from Greenock to Virginia with bale goods, 13.5.1751.
#178	Walter Turnbull, an English master in Hawick, guilty of assaulting the family of the minister of Hawick, was taken to Edinburgh for transportation, 5.1751.
#179	Houston, Douglas, arrived in Romney from St Kitts 5.1751; Betty, Warden, arrived in Greenock from Maryland while William,McLean, arrived from Virginia, both with tobacco, 25.5.1751.
#180	James, Campbell, arrived in Greenock from Virginia and Maryland with tobacco, 1.6.1751; Ann of Aberdeen, Clark, arrived in Aberdeen from Virginia with tobacco, 6.1751.
#181	Matty, Crawford, arrived from Boston with oil, and Cassandra, Hutchison, arrived from Jamaica with sugar, while Graemie, Hunter, sailed to Virginia with bale goods, Greenock 8.6.1751.
#182	Laetitia, Wall, from Aberdeen to Barbados ; Peggy and Nelly, Boyd, arrived in Aberdeen from Maryland with tobacco, 6.1751.
#183	Blackburn, Tran, from Greenock to Virginia with bale goods 22.6.1751.
#184	Annabella, Knox, from Greenock to Virginia with bale goods 29.6.1751.
#185	Greenock, 6.7.1751. Fair Susannah, Strachan, and Port Glasgow, arrived from Carolina with pitch and tar; Scott, Ewing, and Prince William, Smith, arrived from Virginia with tobacco; and Betty, Warden, sailed to Maryland with bale goods.

#187   Glasgow, 22.7.1751. "Robert Dinwiddie Esq., (a native of this city) is appointed Governor and Commander in Chief of HM Colony and Dominion of Virginia."

Thomas Gray, Christian Duncan and Thomas Brown were banished to the American Plantations for 14 years, at Edinburgh 7.1751.

#189   Greenock, 3.8.1751. Mary, MacMillan arrived from Jamaica with sugar, and Ann and Jean, Giddings, arrived from New England with timber

William Harris, guilty of fraud, was banished, and Agnes McCoul or McDoual, guilty of child murder, was ordered to be transported, at Perth 7.1751.

An extract from a letter from Boston reporting a massacre at a village in Nova Scotia in May 1751.

Fanny and Betty, Thomson, and The Jean and Elizabeth, Smith, from Aberdeen to Virginia 8.1751.

#190   Greenock, 12.8.1751. Betty, Maxwell, arrived from Antigua with sugar, and James, Campbell, sailed to Virginia with bale goods.

#191   Greenock, 17.8.1751. Diligence, Aitken, arrived from Jamaica with sugar.

Shirlee of London, Allan, at Stromness 7.1751 with Palatines bound for Philadelphia.

#192   Greenock, 24.8.1751. Kingston, Chisholm, arrived from St Kitts with sugar.

"The good new snow The Antigua Packet of Aberdeen, Lewis Gellie commander, will sail precisely the 16th instant for Cork and Antigua. Any good tradesmen or others who choose to indent for Antigua will meet with suitable encouragement on applying to Captain Gellie or the owners - good accommodation for passengers" 9.1751.

"On Wednesday last George Burnet and Elizabeth Cruickshank were put on board a vessel for Virginia, according to their sentence."

Fanny and Betty of Aberdeen, Thomson, sailed from Aberdeen to Virginia, 9.1751.

#193   Greenock, 31.8.1751. The Montrose, Graham, arrived from Antigua with sugar, while the Cassandra, Hutcheon, sailed to Jamaica with coal.

#194   Greenock, 9.9.1751. The Fair Susanna, Strachan, and The Crauford, Wyllie, sailed to Carolina with bale goods and coal.

Edward Reynolds, from Jamaica, an apprentice surgeon, died in Edinburgh 9.1751.

Finlay Finlayson, from Ross-shire, a thief, was banished, at Edinburgh 4.9.1751, while Margaret Joss, from Banffshire, a child murderer, was banished to the Plantations for life, at Aberdeen 9.1751.

#195 Greenock 14.9.1751 Clyde Boyd, the Susanna Laing, the Joanna Sempill, the Hawk Hastie, arrived from Virginia with tobacco.

#196 Silvy of Hull, Robertson, from Stromness to Virginia. Betty and Sarah Maxwell, from Greenock to Antigua, and Molly Crawford, from Greenock to Boston with bale goods; Argyll, Montgomerie, arrived in the Clyde from St Kitts with sugar, while Margaret Crawford, Dreghorn, Andrew, Boyd Campbell, Friendship Paterson, and Dunlop Alexander, arrived in the Clyde from Virginia with tobacco, 9.1751.

#197 Industry, Cowan, from Leith via Lisbon to South Carolina 10.1751; Margaret Crawford, Boyd Campbell, Dunlop Alexander, Nelly Galbraith, Grizle White, Jeannie Douglas, and Friendship Paterson, arrived in Greenock from Virginia with tobacco, while Argyll Montgomerie, arrived from Antigua with sugar, 28.9.1751; Anne of Aberdeen, Thomson, arrived in Aberdeen from Virginia; Antigua Packet, Gellie, from Aberdeen to Antigua, 10.1751.

#198 "Wanted. A mason and square wright or joiner to go to Jamaica, upon indenting for four years, they shall at least get each £30 per annum and be maintained at bed and board during the time. Any who inclines may commune with John Alexander, writer in Aberdeen, who will engage them with a gentleman of an equal good character and business as any in the island." 15.10.1751.

#198 Adventure of Aberdeen Melvin, arrived in Aberdeen from Virginia, 10.1751.

#199 Two Brothers of Fraserburgh, Elmslie, from Antigua to Holland, sailed from Stromness, while the Fanny and Betty of Aberdeen, Thomson, for Virginia was at Stromness, 10.9.1751; Binning, Steil, arrived in Greenock from Virginia, while the Thetis Andrew, sailed via Cork to Jamaica with staves etc, and the Advice

16

Woodrop, sailed for Virginia with bale goods, 12.10.1751.

Janet Bone, child murderer, was banished to the Plantations for life, and Thomas Campbell, smuggler, was whipped through the streets and banished to the Plantations for life, at Ayr, 10.1751.

#200   Edinburgh, Lyon, from Greenock to the Carolinas with coal etc 19.10.1751; Fanny and Betty, Thomson, from Aberdeen to Virginia, sailed from Stromness 23.9.1751.

"That any young man who is bred to his book and has a good education, so as he is qualified for teaching gentlemen's children Latin, Writing and Arithmetic, and means to officiate in that way in Virginia may apply to Charles Copland jr., merchant in Aberdeen, who has a commission for that purpose and will commune with them upon particulars and give them all proper encouragement, according to his instructions." 29.10.1751.

#201   Houstoun Douglas, and the Montrose Graham, from Greenock to Antigua, while the Duke Jamieson, sailed from Greenock to South Carolina, all with bale goods, 5.11.1751.

#203   Mary, Colquhoun, and the President, Dunlop, arrived in Greenock from Virginia with tobacco, while the Industry Warden, arrived in Greenock from St Kitts with sugar and rum, and the Glasgow McCunn, arrived in Greenock from Boston with tar, 9.11.1751.

John Forrester, a forger, was banished to the Plantations for life, at Edinburgh 11.1751.

#204   Donald Andrew, arrived in Greenock from Virginia, 10.11.1751, while the Mary Dundas, the Duke of Cumberland Dunlop, and the Greenock McCunn, arrived from Virginia 16.11.1751, all with tobacco; Leathly of Aberdeen Lickly, arrived in Aberdeen from Maryland with tobacco 11.1751.

Samuel Lampo, a native of Yorkshire, and a shipmaster in Leith, guilty of shipwrecking, was banished to the Plantations for life by the High Court of the Admiralty in Edinburgh 11.1751.

#205   Bogle, Fleming, the Blackburn, Tran, the Robert, Watson, the Thistle, Coulter, the Mary Shannon, and the Cochran, Steil, arrived in Greenock from Virginia with tobacco,

23.11.1751; Thistle, John Boyd, arrived in Leith from Virginia with tobacco 28.11.1751.

#206   Dunlop, Alexander, from Greenock to South Carolina with merchant goods, 30.11.1751.

#207   Jean and Betty, Smith, from Greenock to St Kitts, the Spencer, Hyndman, and the Susannah, Laing, both from Greenock to Barbados, all with herring, 7.12.1751; Murdoch, Hamilton arrived in Nova Scotia from Holland with Palatines; Charming Lilly, Douglas, arrived at Cromarty from Virginia, 12.1751.

#208   Jean and Mary, Rogers, arrived in Greenock from Virginia with tobacco 14.12.1751; Susannah, King, from Greenock to Cork and the West Indies with herring, 14.12.1751; Newall, Smith, from Greenock to Maryland with bale-goods, 14.12.1751.

"Whereas Alexander Low, merchant in Fraserburgh, is precisely to sail from the Port of Aberdeen for Antigua on or before the 15th February next and proposes to take along with him proper tradesmen and some few servants, to all of whom he will give extraordinary allowances and encouragement particularly to bricklayers, masons, stonecutters, blacksmiths, farriers, cabinetmakers, joiners, tanners, shoemakers. To all of whom if they know their business sufficiently he will give them 10 to 20 pounds sterling yearly besides bed, board, washing and clothing with all other necessaries for the space of 4 years during which space they must enter into indentures with the said Alexander Low, and if any person incline to accept of the above proposals may apply to Mr William Mowat, merchant in Aberdeen, or said Alexander Low merchant at his house in Fraserburgh and as Alexander Low wants but a few and goes along with them himself they may depend on meeting with better than ordinary usage and good accommodation on their passage." 24.12.1751.

#210   Graemy of Glasgow when returning from Virginia was stranded in Dundalk Bay, Ireland; Anderson, Campbell, and the Betty, ..., arrived in Loch Ryan from Virginia with tobacco 28.12.1751; Britannia, Jeffrey, arrived in Greenock from Virginia with tobacco 28.12.1751.

#211   Hall, McMillan, from Greenock to Jamaica with herring 4.1.1752.

#212　　　St Andrew of Aberdeen, Coupar, arrived in Montrose from
　　　　　　　　Virginia 1.1752; Stewart, Williamson, from Greenock to
　　　　　　　　North Carolina with bale goods 18.1.1752.

#214　　　Neptune, Weir, arrived in Lamlash from Philadelphia, and the
　　　　　　　　Dennistoun, Carnegie, arrived in Glasgow from Bristol
　　　　　　　　and Virginia; Argyll, Montgomerie, from Greenock to St
　　　　　　　　Kitts with bale goods, 2 1752

#215　　　Polly, Ramsay, from Carolina with tar, the Neptune, Weir,
　　　　　　　　from Philadelphia, the James and David, Scott, from
　　　　　　　　Boston with timber, the Bowling, Campbell, from Virginia
　　　　　　　　with tobacco, all arrived in Greenock 1.2.1752;
　　　　　　　　St Andrew of Aberdeen, Cooper, arrived in Aberdeen
　　　　　　　　from Virginia with tobacco 2.1752.

#216　　　Pearl, Frances, from Virginia with tobacco, the Peggie, Yuill,
　　　　　　　　from Boston with timber, arrived in Greenock 8.2.1752;
　　　　　　　　Jenny, Aitken, and the Mary, Crawford, from Greenock
　　　　　　　　to Jamaica with herring, 8.2.1752; Margaret, Crawford,
　　　　　　　　from Greenock to Virginia with bale-goods, 8.2.1752.

#217　　　Grizel of Irvine, Ewing, from the West Indies was wrecked 70
　　　　　　　　leagues off Ireland when she struck a whale.

　　　　　　　　Nancy, Gray, the Rowand, Mitchell, the Betty, Hughs, and the
　　　　　　　　Murdoch, Hamilton, arrived in Greenock from Virginia
　　　　　　　　with tobacco 17.2.1752; Caledonia of Aberdeen, Harvie,
　　　　　　　　arrived in Aberdeen from Virginia with tobacco 2.1752.

#218　　　Leith Galley, Charles Thomason, arrived in Burntisland from
　　　　　　　　Jamaica 3.3.1752; Industry of Aberdeen, Ross, from
　　　　　　　　Aberdeen to Antigua 3.3.1752.

#219　　　Rowand, Mitchell, the Nancy, Gray, the Betty, Hughs, and the
　　　　　　　　Murdoch, Hamilton, all arrived in Greenock from Virginia
　　　　　　　　with tobacco 2.3.1752.
　　　　　　　　"For Kingston in Jamaica, the Laurel of Aberdeen,
　　　　　　　　　　commander John Coutts, who sails the 15th April next
　　　　　　　　wind and weather permitting. Any gentlemen or ladies
　　　　　　　　who have any goods to ship or want to go as
　　　　　　　　passengers may be accommodated on very reasonable
　　　　　　　　terms. NB the ship touches at London on the way to
　　　　　　　　Jamaica." 10.3.1752.

#220　　　Leith Galley, Thomson, arrived at Leith from Jamaica
　　　　　　　　9.3.1752.
　　　　　　　　Diligence of Aberdeen, Duncan, from Aberdeen to Antigua,
　　　　　　　　3.1752.

#221	Antigua Packet of Aberdeen, Gellie, arrived in Antigua from Aberdeen.
	Buchanan Hunter, the Robert Watson, and Donald Andrew, from Greenock to Virginia with bale goods, 21.3.1752. Peggy and Nelly Boyd, Industry Warden, Kingston Chisholm, the May Crawford, and Clyde Boyd, from Greenock to the West Indies with herring and bale goods 21.3.1752.
	Arbroath, Gellatly, from Virginia to Montrose was lost at sea and the crew of 4 drowned, 3.1752.
#222	St Andrew master Robert Donaldson, arrived at Leith from New York with lintseed, oil, and staves, 4.1752.
	Industry of Aberdeen, Ross, and the Diligence of Aberdeen, Duncan, from Aberdeen to Antigua 3.1752.
#223	Hawk Hastie, the Blackburn Graham, the Duke of Cumberland Dunlop, and the Greenock McCunn, from Greenock to Virginia with bale goods 28.3.1752.
	Industry of Leith Captain Andrew Cowan, arrived at Charleston, South Carolina, 4.2.1752 with all passengers and crew in good health.
	Aberdeen 7.4.1752 - "On Wednesday Margaret Joass was put aboard a ship bound for Virginia, pursuant to sentence of transportation passed on her last Circuit."
#224	Ann of Aberdeen, Thomson, from Aberdeen to Virginia with bale goods 4.1752.
	Kennedy Gillies, from Greenock to Barbados, the Dennistoun Carnegie, from Greenock to Virginia, and the Glasgow Campbell, from Greenock to Boston, all with bale goods 4.4.1752.
	Jamaica Packet, Alexander Glassfoord, from Leith via Madeira to Jamaica 4.1752.
#226	Brothers Alexander, from Greenock to Barbados, and the Mary Shannon, from Greenock to Virginia with bale goods 20.4.1752.
	William Jack, thief and housebreaker, was banished to the Plantations for life, Grizel Stuart and Elizabeth Ross, guilty of child murder, successfully petitioned for transportation and banishment for life, David Goodwillie, a thief and forger, was sentenced to be whipped through the streets of Cupar and then banished for life at Perth 13.4.1752. David Swan, a thief, successfully petitioned for transportation, at Dumfries 4.1752. Charles Brydie, a

thief, was banished to the Plantations in America, at
Aberdeen 4.1752.

Laurel Coutts, from Aberdeen to Jamaica 4.1752.

#227 Grizel White, and Advice Wardrop, arrived at Greenock
from Virginia, Eglinton McAuslan, arrived in South
Carolina from the Clyde, Dunlop Alexander, arrived at
Cowes from South Carolina, Concord Aitken, arrived at
Ayr from Virginia, the Thistle Coulter, the Britannia ....,
and Nancy Gray, from Greenock to Virginia with bale
goods, and two other ships arrived in Greenock from
New England with lintseed, lumber, and oil, 4.1752.

Jean and Elizabeth of Aberdeen, Smith, arrived in Aberdeen
from Virginia with tobacco, 5.1752.

#228 Duke Jamieson, arrived in Greenock from Lisbon and South
Carolina with wine and fruit, 5.1752.

James Campbell, arrived in Greenock from Virginia with
tobacco, and Ann Orr, arrived in Greenock from
Boston with lumber, and Jean Motherwell, from
Greenock to Virginia with bale goods, 5.1752

John Stuart, Jean Wilson, Joseph and Peter Stuart, indicted
for theft, and Anne Chalmers for child murder, petitioned
for banishment, which was granted at Ayr 25.4.1752.

#229 Menie Montgomerie, and Mary Dundas, from Greenock to
Virginia with bale goods, 9.5.1752.

Patrick Fisher, for the theft of a tartan plaid, was banished to
the Plantations for life, at Stirling 2.5.1752, [AJ#229]

#230 Jean and Betty Smith, arrived in the Clyde from St Kitts with
sugar, 18.5.1752.

#231 Jenny Cunningham, arrived in Greenock from Virginia with
tobacco, 5.1752.

#232 Houstoun of Glasgow, arrived in London from St Kitts
5.6.1752.

Fanny and Betty of Aberdeen, Thomson, arrived in Aberdeen
from Virginia with tobacco, while the Leathly of
Aberdeen, Likely, sailed from Aberdeen to Virginia with
merchandise, 6.1752.

#233 Jean and Mary, Rodger, Dreghorn, Andrew, and
Neptune Weir, from Greenock to Virginia with bale
goods, 6.1752.

#234 Betty and Sally, Maxwell, arrived in Greenock from Antigua
with sugar 13.6.1752, while Peggy Yuill, sailed from
Greenock to Boston, and Murdoch, Hamilton, and

Duke, Jamieson, sailed from Greenock to Virginia with bale goods, 6.1752.

Glasgow, 15.6.1752. "On Thursday several persons who were indicted for theft at the May Circuit in Ayr and were allowed banishment on petition, were brought in hither under a military guard in order to their being transported to the Plantations, and on Saturday these with 14 others, were sent to Greenock in order to be shipped to Virginia."

#234 Cassandra, Hutchison, arrived in Greenock from Jamaica with sugar, and Jean, How, arrived in Greenock from Virginia with tobacco, 30.6.1752.

#236 Fair Susanna, Captain Strachan, belonging to Mr George Forbes, a merchant in Edinburgh, from Leith to South Carolina 6.1752.

"After a passage of 7 weeks the Methven of Glasgow, Coppel, arrived at Manna on the Windward Coast of Guinea December 11, he had began to purchase Negroes and was to touch at any place of trade from Cape Palmas to Anamboo till his number was complete."

Amity Reid, arrived at Ayr from Virginia, while the Binning Steel, the Grizel White, the Advice Wardrop, and the Lilly Somerville, arrived in Greenock from Virginia, and Duke of Argyll, King, sailed from Greenock to Virginia with bale goods 27.6.1752.

"We hear that about 60 families, mostly from Kilmaurs, are embarking on board a vessel in Saltcoats for Pennsylvania in order to go and settle there."

#238 Jean and Betty, from Greenock to St Kitts with bale goods 13.7.1752, while Margaret, Crawford, Boyd, Douglas, and Blackburn, Graham, arrived in Greenock from Virginia with tobacco 7.1752.

"On Friday Charles Brodie jr. was, pursuant to his sentence at the last circuit, put aboard a vessel bound to Virginia." 21.7.1752.

#240 Glasgow, Campbell, arrived in Boston from the Clyde, Mally, Crawford, arrived in Greenock from Virginia with tobacco and Stewart, Williamson, arrived in Greenock from North Carolina with pitch and tar, 25.7.1752, Ann, Orr, from Greenock to Virginia with bale goods, Lovely Susan, Strachan, from Leith to South Carolina with wine and bale goods, St Andrew, Elmslie, from Aberdeen to Virginia with bale goods, 7.1752.

"On Saturday John Grant and John Lyon from Forfar who had petitioned the Sheriff of Angus for banishment, were shipped off from this place to Virginia." Aberdeen, 4.8.1752.

#241 Nelly, Galbraith, arrived in Greenock from Virginia with tobacco 1.8.1752.

Betsy and Sally, Maxwell, from Greenock to Antigua with bale goods 8.1752.

Andrew Ross, from Glasgow, a merchant in Virginia, went aboard a convict ship from London caught gaol distemper and died in a few days.

#243 Friendship of Ayr, arrived in Ayr from Virginia 17.8.1752, Montrose, Graham, arrived in Greenock from St Kitts with sugar 15.8.1752, and Robert, Watson, and Susie, King, arrived in Greenock from Virginia with tobacco 15.8.1752.

#245 Hawk, Hastie, arrived in Greenock from Maryland with tobacco, while Jenny Cunningham, and Glencairn, Glasgow, from Greenock to Virginia with bale goods, and Cassandra, Hutcheson, from Greenock to Philadelphia and Jamaica with bale goods, 29.8.1751.

#245 "A snow, name unknown, from Carolina to Leith, is lost to the northwards of Shields." 19.9.1752

#246 Glasgow, 18.9.1752. "We have advice that one of the Montrose Guineamen is arrived in the Potomac River, Virginia, consigned to Mr William Black. The sale of Negro men at £32 and for women £30 sterling, the country duty paid by the purchaser..".

Duke of Cumberland, Dunlop, Port Glasgow, McClintock, Clyde, Boyd, Donald, Andrew, Greenock, Morison, arrived in Greenock from Virginia with tobacco 9.1752.

William Douglas and Janet MacLaren, adulterers, banished at Stirling 9.1752, he from Scotland for 3 years and she to the Plantations for life. James Smith, a thief, petitioned successfully to be transported to America, and William Ferguson, a rioter, banished for 7 years, at Ayr 9.1752.

#247 Glasgow, Campbell from Boston with pitch and tar, Kingston, Chisholm, from St Kitts with sugar, Argyll, Montgomery, from Antigua with sugar, and Richard and

23

Mary, Coats, from Piscatqua with lumber, arrived at Greenock 28.9.1752.

#248   Matty, Orr, arrived in Greenock from Virginia with tobacco 10.1752.

#248   John Turner, thief, banished to the Plantations for life, at Glasgow 10.10.1752; John Bain, sheep thief, transported for life, Angus McPhie, cow thief, banished to the Plantations, Kenneth and Donald McWilliams, cowthieves, banished to the Plantations for life, David and George Ross, cow thieves, banished to the Plantations for 7 years, at Inverness 21.9.1752; George Galdie and Andrew Milne, thieves, and George Gordon, forger, banished to the Plantations, at Aberdeen 9.1752.

#250   Elizabeth, Morrison, to Virginia, and Montrose, Graham, to St Kitts, from Greenock with bale goods 13.10.1752.

William Parker, a former soldier of Rich's Regiment, who had been found guilty of forging bank-notes and transported to America, was arrested in Edinburgh and committed to the Tolbooth, 10.1752.

#251   Buchanan, Hunter, arrived in Greenock from Virginia with tobacco, and the Lilly, Somervill, from Greenock to Virginia with bale goods, 31.10.1752.

William Parker, who was sentenced in June 1751 to banishment to Boston, New England, for life {see above} was to be whipped on the first market day of each month until a ship is found to return him to the Plantations, Edinburgh 31.10.1752.

#252   Industry, Andrew Cowan, from Leith to South Carolina, 10.1752, and Susannah, Laing, arrived at Greenock from Virginia with tobacco.

#253   Montgomerie, Dunlop, Mary, Shannon, and Cochrane, Semple, arrived in Greenock from Virginia with tobacco, while James, Wotherspoon, from Greenock to St Martin's, West Indies, with bale goods, 4.11.1752.

James Low, tenant in Easthill of Johnston, thief in Stonehaven Tolbooth, was banished to the Plantations in America 11.1752.

Ann, Thomson, arrived in Aberdeen from Virginia with tobacco 11.1752.

#254   Scott, Ewing, and the Mary, Dundas, arrived in Greenock from Virginia with tobacco 21.11.1752.

#255   Wilmington, Hugh Walker, arrived in Leith from North
Carolina with tar and pitch, 28.11.1752.
Jeanie, Douglas, and the Carey, Brown, arrived in Greenock
from Virginia with tobacco 11.1752.
Leathly of Aberdeen, Lickly, arrived in Aberdeen from
Maryland, 11.1752.

#256   Jean, Motherwell, and the Dennistoun, Carnegie, arrived in
Greenock from Virginia with tobacco; while the
Glasgow, Campbell, sailed from Greenock to Boston
with bale goods, 11.1752.

#257   James Peacock, son of John Peacock in Glasgow, a mariner
based in Havanna, sailed via Cape Horn to Japan in 4
months 14 days and returned via the Cape of Good
Hope in 3 months 23 days.

#258   Catherine, Jamieson, from Boston with lumber, the Dreghorn,
Andrew, and the Joanna, Wardrop, from Virginia with
tobacco, arrived in Glasgow; while the Duke of
Cumberland, Dunlop, from Greenock to Virginia with
bale goods 12.1752.
Potomac Merchant, Hartley, arrived in Montrose from
Maryland and Virginia with tobacco, staves, etc and
from Guinea gold dust and elephants' teeth, 12.1752.

#259   Hope of Montrose, Dunbar, arrived in Montrose from Salem,
New England, with wood, tar, pitch and turpentine.
12.1752.

#260   Thistle of Glasgow, Coulter, from Virginia with tobacco was
stranded near Rye 2.1753.
Bowling, Campbell, and the Betty, Warden, arrived at
Greenock from Virginia with tobacco, and the Industry,
Warden, arrived at Greenock from St Kitts with sugar
and tobacco, 2.1753.
"For Antigua. Against the first of February next the good ship
the Antigua Packet, Lewis Gellie commander, where
there is good accommodation for passengers,
tradesmen and servants of good character will be
indented on the best terms upon   applying to John
Elphinstone or Andrew Garioch, merchants in
Aberdeen, owners of the said ship." 2.2.1753.

#261   Brothers of Ayr from Virginia to Ayr with tobacco was
wrecked near Portnaferry, Ireland; the Nancy of
Glasgow, Gray, from Maryland with tobacco was
beached off Kirkcudbright; the Rowand of Glasgow,

Tran, arrived in South Carolina from Holland with Palatines; the James and David, Scott, arrived in Greenock from Virginia with tobacco; the Caledonia, Currie, arrived in Glasgow from Boston, the Caesar, Wylie, from Greenock to Jamaica; and the Caledonia of Aberdeen, Hervie, arrived in Charleston, South Carolina, 1.1753.

#262 Susie, King, from Greenock to Antigua with herring 6.1.1753, the Binning arrived in Greenock from Virginia with tobacco, the Leathly of Aberdeen, Lickly, arrived in Aberdeen from Maryland with tobacco, 1.1753.

#263 Duke of Argyll, King, from Virginia with tobacco, the Jenny, Cunningham, and the President, Dunlop, both from Philadelphia, arrived at Greenock 14.1.1753.

A vessel from Boston, New England, to Montrose was stranded on the Flemish coast, 1.1753.

St Andrew of Aberdeen, Elmslie, arrived in Aberdeen from Virginia with tobacco, 1.1753.

#264 Murdoch, Hamilton, the Anderson, Campbell, the Bess, Scott, and the Anne, Orr, arrived in Greenock from Virginia with tobacco 29.1.1753; the Thistle Boyd, arrived in Leith from Virginia with tobacco 30.1.1753; and the Jean and Elizabeth, Smith, arrived in Aberdeen from Virginia, 1.1753.

#265 Margaret, Crawford, arrived in Greenock from Virginia with tobacco 1.1753.

#266 Aberdeen 13.2.1753. "Yesterday George Gordon, George Gauldie and Andrew Milne were put on board the Planter, Captain Alexander Ogilvie commander, who sailed from this port for Virginia ... as also John Low, from the Mearns, who petitioned for banishment and had it granted."

Planter, Ogilvie, from Aberdeen to Virginia 12.2.1753.

#267 Susannah, Laing, and the Industry, Warden, from Greenock to St Kitts with herring 6.2.1753.

#268 Dinwiddie, formerly the President, Dunlop, the Jean and Mary, Rodger, arrived in Greenock from Virginia with tobacco 2.1753.

#269 Dinwoodie, Dunlop, the Kennedy, ..., and the Jean, How, arrived in Greenock from Virginia with tobacco 24.2.1753.

#270   Hartwood, Kennan, arrived in Greenock from Virginia with tobacco, and the Dennistoun, Carnegie, and the Falmouth, Addison, from Greenock to Virginia with bale goods, 3.3.1753.

#270   James Smith, a carrier in Galashiels, guilty of forgery, was sentenced to be pilloried, imprisoned and then transported to America, 3.1753.

#270   Mercury of Montrose, Moodie, and the Jean and Elizabeth of Aberdeen, Smith, arrived in Aberdeen from Virginia with tobacco 3.1753.

#271   Donald, Andrew, and the Prince William, Donald, from Greenock to Virginia with bale goods 10.3.1753.

#272   Industry of Leith, Andrew Cowan, arrived in Charleston, South Carolina, 24.1.1753.

#273   Planter, arrived in Leith from Jamaica with mahogany and sugar, while the Forth arrived in Leith from Virginia with tobacco, 27.3.1753; the Glencairn, Campbell arrived in Boston from the Clyde 30.1.1753.

#274   Amity, Reid, arrived in Greenock from Virginia with tobacco, while the James, Manderston, sailed from Greenock to Virginia, 31.3.1753.

#275   Cary, Brown, Margaret, Crawford, Menie, Thomson, Mary, Shannon, Crawford, Barton, and the Buchanan, Rae, from Greenock to Virginia with bale goods 7.4.1753; while the Jean, Melvin, arrived in Leith from Newport in America with flaxseed 12.4.1753; and the Brittania, Orr, from Greenock to Virginia with balegoods 14.4.1753.

#276   James Marjorybanks, a forger, and William Muir, a housebreaker and thief, petitioned to be transported for life, which was granted, at Dumfries 4.1753.

#277   Pearl, Francis, arrived in Greenock from Virginia with tobacco 22.4.1753.

#277   '16 prisoners in Edinburgh Tolbooth who had indented for Virginia, were transported thence to Leith and put upon the Thistle, Boyd, for that place 22.4.1753.'

#278   Peggy, Youl, Anderson, Campbell, and Bowling, Campbell, from Greenock to Virginia with bale goods, Caledonia, Curry, from Greenock to Boston with bale goods, and the Jean and Betty, Smith, from Greenock to St Kitts with herring 28.4.1753.

#279   Cathcart, Buchanan, from Greenock to Virginia 5.5.1753.

#280	Mary, Hamilton, Neptune, Weir, Grizzle, White, Glencairn, Glasgow, Jean, Motherwell, and Rebecca, Clark, from Greenock to Virginia with bale goods 12.5.1753.
#280	Jean Imlay, James Middleton, Alexander Martin, and John Craig, thieves, petitioned for transportation which was granted, at Aberdeen 5.1753.
#281	Murdoch, Hamilton, from Greenock to Virginia with balegoods 19.5.1753, while the Dolphin of Dundee, Glass, arrived in Perth from Jamaica with wine, sugar, cotton, mahogany, etc.; Pearl of Montrose, McCowan, arrived in Montrose from Virginia and Maryland with tobacco, and the Thistle, Murray, was at Stromness 3.5.1753 on way from Leith to Virginia.
#283	'The Hudson Bay Company ships that recently sailed, not having a sufficient number of forces for their settlements abroad, are at the Orkneys to complete their complement of men and then proceed on their intended voyage.' 31.5.1753.
#283	Industry, Andrew Cowan, arrived at Leith from Charleston, South Carolina, in 7 weeks with ship tar, pitch, turpentine, rice, mahogany, staves, and deerskins, 1.6.1753; and the Kennedy Walker, sailed from Greenock to Virginia with bale goods 2.6.1753.
#284	Cassandra, Gray, arrived at Greenock from Jamaica with sugar and cotton, Jeanny, Cunningham, arrived at Greenock from Virginia with tobacco, and the Duke of Cumberland, Dunlop, sailed from Greenock to Virginia with bale goods, 19.6.1753.
#284	"For London and Kingston in Jamaica, the ship Augustus Caesar of Aberdeen, Captain John Coutts commander, now lying in this harbor will sail positively the 16th inst. Any who incline to ship goods or go as passenger may treat with the Captain every day at the Exchange or at the Coffee Houses. Great encouragement is given to young men who incline to engage as servants for the space of 4 years."
#285	Thetis, Andrew, and Lilly, Somerville, arrived in Greenock from Virginia with tobacco; Amity, Reid, and Nelly, Galbraith, from Greenock to Virginia with balegoods, and Montgomery, Dunlop, from Greenock to Jamaica with herring, 26.6.1753.

#286   Houston, Douglas, arrived in Greenock from St Kitts with
sugar, 3.7.1753; Adventure of Aberdeen, Melvin, from
Campvere to Maryland, foundered near Island Flores
11.5.1753, the captain and the crew were taken on a
brig from North Carolina to Fyall; Augustus Caesar,
Coutts, sailed from Aberdeen to Jamaica with bale
goods etc

#288   Montrose, Graham, arrived in Greenock from St Kitts with
sugar 9.7.1753; Elizabeth and Peggy of Leith, Scott,
was at Stromness 21.6.1753 on way from Leith to
Carolina, it later sailed 23.6.1753; and the Neptune,
Dunbar, sailed from Montrose to Boston with wine and
sailcloth 7.1753.

#289   St Mungo, Hall, arrived in Greenock from Antigua with sugar
16.7.1753.

#290   Binning, Steel, arrived in Greenock from Virginia with tobacco
20.7.1753.

#291   Stewart of Greenock, a brigantine, Williamson, arrived in Leith
from North Carolina with pitch, turpentine and tobacco;
the Friendship, arrived in Ayr from Virginia; the Hope,
Moodie, arrived in Aberdeen from Montrose bound for
Virginia; and the Duke of Argyll, King, sailed from
Greenock to Virginia with bale goods, 7.1753.

#293   Eglinton, McAuslan, Susie, King, Boyd, Douglas, Cary, Brown,
Donald, Andrew, Port Glasgow, McLintock, arrived in
Greenock from Virginia, and the Joanna, Coulter, sailed
from Greenock to Boston with bale goods, 11.8.1753.
Charming Nancy, George Forbes, arrived in Leith from
South Carolina with rice, tar, pitch, and mahogony,
8.1753.
"The following persons were upon petition for banishment,
sentenced to be transported to America, viz. John
Mathie, indicted for coining or uttering false coin, to be
transported for life, ... Donaldson, for uttering false coin,
for 7 years, and .... Taylor, for counterfeiting a banknote,
for 5 years." at Edinburgh 8.1753.

#294   James and Alexander, Wotherspoon, arrived in the Clyde
from the West Indies 8.1753; Princess Louisa, Gardner,
arrived in Greenock from Philadelphia with tar
18.8.1753; Montrose, Graham, from Greenock to St
Kitts and the Jenny, Paterson, from Greenock to
Virginia both with bale goods; and the St Andrew,

Coupar, from Aberdeen to Virginia with bale goods, 8.1753.

"On Wednesday Alexander Martin, John Craig, James Middleton and Jean Imlay, were shipped on board a vessel for Virginia."

#295   Blackburn, Graham, Prince William, Donald, Dennistoun, Carnegy, arrived in Greenock from Virginia with tobacco 25.8.1753; Alexander and James, Wotherspoon, arrived in Greenock from the West Indies, Boyd, Body, arrived in Greenock from Montserrat, and Nancy, Body, arrived in Greenock from Jamaica, with cotton, sugar and rum, while the Binning, Steel, sailed from Greenock to Virginia, 8.1753. Trial, Watt, arrived in Aberdeen from Virginia with tobacco, 8.1753.

#296   Kilmaurs, Crawford, Menie, Thomson, Margaret, Crawford, arrived in Greenock from Virginia with tobacco, and the Kingston, Chisholm, arrived in Greenock from St Kitts with sugar and cotton; Industry of Leith, Cowan, from Leith to South Carolina with wine, coal, and bale goods; and the Fanny and Betty of Aberdeen, Thomson, arrived in Virginia from Aberdeen, 9.1753.

#297   Charming Nancy, Byter, arrived at Leith from New York with pitch and tar, and the Celia, Grigg, arrived in Leith from Boston with naval stores; Cochran, Semple, Falmouth, Anderson, Greenock, Robertson, and Anderson, Campbell, arrived in Greenock from Virginia with tobacco, while the Jean and Nancy, Ritchie, arrived in Greenock from St Kitts with sugar, 9.1753.

#299   "Letters received [in Glasgow] by the Caledonia, Captain Currie, from Boston {for which place the said ship we hear is to sail soon} inform, that the persons who went over last harvest and spring are highly pleased with their settlements upon Brigadiers Waldo's land on the St George River ...."   2.10.1753.

John Peacock, indicted for theft, and Anne Earl, indicted for child murder, were banished to the Plantations for life, at Ayr; Rory Dow McDonald in Glengarry, thief, was banished to America for life, at Inverness; while ... Gordon and ...... Hay were banished to America for life, at Aberdeen 9.1753.

#300   Matty, Orr, arrived in Greenock from Virginia with tobacco 29.9.1753.

#301	Charming Nancy of Leith, Murray, at Stromness 16.10.1753, on voyage from Leith to South Carolina with bale goods. Mary, Shannon, and Katherine Jamieson, arrived in Greenock from Virginia with tobacco 6.10.1753.
#302	Jenny, Motherwell, arrived in Greenock from Virginia with tobacco; Alexander and James, Wotherspoon, and Houston, Douglas, from Greenock to the West Indies with bale goods, and Susie, King, from Greenock to Virginia with bale goods, 10.1753.
#303	Industry, Warden, and Jean and Betty, Smith, arrived in Greenock from the West Indies with sugar and cotton 20.10.1753, while the Caledonia, Curry, sailed from Greenock to Boston with bale goods.
#304	Grizie, White, arrived in Greenock from Virginia with tobacco, 6.11.1753. Planter of Aberdeen, Alexander Ogilvie, was stranded on Grahamsay in the Orkneys when sailing from Maryland to Aberdeen with tobacco, tar and turpentine, 16.10.1753.
#305	Isabella, Seaman, from Leith to New York, with coal and bale goods, 5.11.1753; Duke of Cumberland, Dunlop, and Rebecca, Clerk, arrived in Greenock from Virginia with tobacco 3.11.1753.
#306	Buchanan, Rae, and Jeannie, Douglas, arrived in the Clyde from Virginia 12.11.1753.
#307	Buchanan, Rae, Jeannie, Douglas, Bogle, Montgomery, Bowling, Campbell, arrived in Greenock from Virginia with tobacco while Argyll, Montgomery, arrived in Greenock from Antigua with sugar and cotton, 17.11.1753.
#308	United Janets, Robert Forrester, arrived in Leith from New York with naval stores, 12.1753; Planter of Aberdeen, Ogilvie, at Stromness on way to Virginia 11 1753; Murdoch, Hamilton, Britannia, Orr, Scot, Tran, arrived in Greenock from Virginia with tobacco 20.11.1753. Letter from Captain Coulter of Joanna of Glasgow dated 28.9.1753 Piscataqua Bay, New England, stating that the ship with its 60 passengers had arrived safely and that the passengers were to settle on Brigadier Waldo's land on the St George River.
#309	Industry, Warden, from Greenock to Barbados, and Port Glasgow, McLintock, from Greenock to Antigua, both with herring, 1.12.1753.

#310   Thistle of Leith, Murray, arrived in Leith from Virginia with
tobacco; Susannah, Lang, from Greenock to Antigua,
and Mally, Crawford, from Greenock to Barbados, both
with herring, 12.1753.

#311   Kingston, Chisholm, and Mary, Hamilton, from Greenock to St
Kitts with herring, 19.12.1753.

#312   Cathcart, Buchanan, arrived in Greenock from Virginia with
tobacco, and the Greenock, Hill. sailed from Greenock
for Jamaica with herring 22.12.1753.

#313   Jean, Howie, and Dreghorn, Andrew, arrived in Greenock
from Virginia with tobacco, while the Annabella, Knox,
arrived in Greenock from Jamaica with sugar and
cotton, 29.12.1753.

#314   Adventure of Ayr, arrived at Lamlash from Virginia, and the
Brothers, Hunter, arrived in Greenock from Virginia,
5.1.1754. The Industry of Leith, Andrew Cowan, and the
Mercury of Dundee, James Strachan, arrived in
Charleston, South Carolina, after an 8 week crossing.

#315   Duke of Argyll, King, and Betty, Warden, arrived in
Greenock from Virginia with tobacco 12.1.1754.
James Teviotdale, in the parish of Clate, Aberdeenshire, a
prisoner in Stonehaven Tolbooth, accused of horse
theft, petitioned successfully for transportation to
America, 1.1754.

#316   Leith Galley, John Sharp, arrived in Leith from Jamaica with
rum and sugar; Dunlop, Alexander, arrived in
Lochindaal, Islay, from Virginia, and Peggie, Dunlop,
arrived in the Clyde from Virginia, 1.1754.

#317   Hawk, Heastie, arrived in Greenock from Maryland with
tobacco 26.1.1754, while Mary, Brown, sailed from
Greenock to Virginia with bale goods.

#318   Dolphin, Wills, arrived in Greenock from Boston with lumber,
Caesar, Wyllie, from Greenock to Jamaica and
Britannia, Robertson, from Greenock to St Kitts both
with herring, Boyd, Douglas, from Greenock to Virginia
with bale goods, and Jean of Aberdeen, Smith, arrived
in Aberdeen from Virginia with tobacco, 2.1754.

#319   Dunlop, Alexander, and Bedford, Brown, arrived in Greenock
from Virginia with tobacco, while Argyle, Montgomery,
sailed from Greenock to St Kitts with herring and bale
goods, 2.1754.

#320	The schooner Polly, Watt, from Boston, New England, for Leith, was wrecked off St Maloes, France. 2.1754. Donald, Andrew, arrived in Greenock from Virginia with tobacco, and Bachelor, Ewing, arrived in Greenock from Rhode Island, 16.2.1754.
#321	"A vessel from Scotland is arrived at Portsmouth, New Hampshire, with near 300 passengers on board who design to settle there." 5.3.1754.
#322	Pearl, Francis, and Jeannie, Paterson, arrived in Greenock from Virginia with tobacco 2.3.1754; while Cranston, Johnston, arrived in Leith from Cape Fear with tar 4.3.1754.
#323	Margaret, Crawford, and Menie, Thomson, from Greenock to Virginia; Fanny and Betty of Aberdeen, Thomson, and Montrose, Moodie, from Aberdeen to Virginia; while Gordon, Geddes, arrived in Leith from New York with lintseed, 3.1754.
	"On Tuesday last John Gun {who had his sentence of death turned into transportation}, Agnes Taylor, alias Snippy, his wife and Sarah Gun {a young hopeful of 12 years of age} their daughter who did volunteer; William Gordon and John Hay, were all put on board the Fanny and Betty of Aberdeen, Captain Thomson, for Virginia." 19.3.1754.
#325	Royal Widow, Smith, arrived in Greenock from Virginia with tobacco 23.3.1754.
	Walter Robertson in Sandyholes, guilty of reset, was banished to the Plantations for life, at Glasgow, while Donald Morrison, a thief, was banished to the Plantations in America for life, at Edinburgh, 3.1754.
#327	Thistle, Murray, from Leith to Virginia 9.4.1754; Montrose, Graham, arrived in Greenock from St Kitts with sugar; Caledonia, McLeod, arrived in Greenock from Rhode Island with flax seed; Grizle, White, and Duke of Cumberland, Dunlop, sailed from Greenock to Virginia with bale goods, 4.1754.
#328	Peggy, Dunlop, and Alexander and Anne, Clerk, arrived in Greenock from Virginia with tobacco, 4.1754.
	John Cameron, herd to Angus Cameron of Kinlochleven, Donald Dow Og McMarrin alias Cameron late tenant in Braes of Aird, John Dow McConnochy alias McDonald late in Killilan, John Dow McPhail late in Stratherrick,

Simon Fraser late in Stratherrick. who had been indicted of theft, petitioned for banishment to the Plantations, which was granted, while Rory Roy McGory or McDonald in Glengarry, found guilty of theft, was banished for life, at Inverness 4.1754. Thomas Smith elder in Knock, James Crab in Old Deer, who had been indicted for housebreaking, petitioned to be transported to HM Plantations for life, which was granted, at Aberdeen, 4.1754.

#330   Caledonia, Corrie, arrived in Greenock from Boston with flax seed and lumber 27.4.1754; Bedford, Brown, from Greenock to Virginia; while Jean and Betty, Smith, and Montrose, Graham, sailed from Greenock to Jamaica with bale goods, 5.1754.

#331   Janet Foyer, servant to Reverend Duncan McFarlane in Drymen, and Thomas Douglas, a tinker in Bannockburn, who had been indicted for theft, petitioned to be transported to the Plantations, which was granted, at Stirling 5.1754.

Neptune of Montrose, Dunbar, arrived in Aberdeen from Virginia, 5.1754.

#332   John and Archibald, Glasgow, arrived in Greenock from Virginia with tobacco; while Mathie, Orr, sailed from Greenock to Virginia, and Nancy, Morrison, from Greenock to Boston, both with bale goods, 11.5.1754.

John Stark, indicted for theft, successfully petitioned to be transported, in Edinburgh 6.5.1754.

#333   Ann, Cuthbert, arrived in Greenock from Maryland with tobacco 5.1754.

"For Antigua and Jamaica. A good large ship {the 150 tons Planter} to sail from Aberdeen by 20th July next. Therefore all men servants from 12 to 40 years old will be indentured for the said islands upon applying to John Elphinstone or Andrew Garioch, merchants in Aberdeen, and as there will go along with the ship one well acquainted in the islands the servants may depend on good usage and be provided in humane masters. For further particulars refer to the advertisement published the 24th inst. NB there will be good accommodation for passengers. Tradesmen qualified in their business, of a good character will get reasonable encouragement by yearly wages but they indenture no convicts nor those

addicted to thieving and drinking. Any qualified
surgeons going to those islands for business will get
a reasonable reward for taking care of the crew and
servants at sea." 28.5.1754.

#335   "last week sailed from Greenock to Virginia the Pearl, Francis,
having on board Walter Rutherford of Sandyholes, ...
Armstrong, ... McLeish, and about 28 others of both
sexes from prison in Glasgow. It is hoped that the
change of climate will have the desired effect of making
those idle and abandoned creatures useful members of
society." 11.6.1754.

Hope of Aberdeen, Mudie, from Aberdeen to Virginia 6.1754.

#336   Sally, Russell, and the Cary, Brown, arrived in Greenock from
Virginia with sugar, rum and tobacco, 18.6.1754.

"7 men were brought to Glasgow prison from Inverness in
order for transportation to America in pursuance of their
sentence at the last Circuit Court in that place."
6.5.1754.

#337   Cassandra, Hutcheon, arrived in Port Glasgow from Jamaica
with sugar, and Nelly, Galbraith, arrived in Greenock f
rom   Virginia with tobacco, 25.6.1754.

Grizie, John Cameron, from Saltcoats to Philadelphia with 140
passengers. 6.1754.

"For Kingston in Jamaica. The Augustus Caesar, John Coutts
commander, who will positively sail from this port 20th
August next. Any gentleman, ladies, or others who want
to ship goods or go passenger, may treat with the said
commander on very reasonable terms, he having fine
accommodation for passengers; and any young men,
milnwrights, joiners, masons or others who will engage
themselves for 4 years service shall meet with the
greatest encouragement and make sure of good
masters and even their indentures to be delivered to
them upon finding any persons to pay their passage on
their arrival there. In Captain Coutts absence enquire at
John Leslie, merchant in the Green, Aberdeen."
25.6.1754.

#338   Mercury, Strachan, from Leith to South Carolina, and Forth,
Brown, from Leith to Virginia, 25.6.1754.

#339   Wilmington, Murray, arrived in Leith from North Carolina, with
tar 9.7.1754.

Letter, dated 29.5.1754, from a gentleman in Port Royal, Virginia, to a correspondent in Aberdeen regarding the expedition led by Colonel Fry and George Washington against the French.

#340   Prince William, Donald, arrived in Greenock fromVirginia with tobacco 16.7.1754.

James McKirdy, a farmer, plus Alexander and Thomas Hamilton in Arran, prisoners in Edinburgh Tolbooth, indicted of assaulting a Customs officer, were banished to HM Plantations in America for life, at Edinburgh 7.1754.

#341   Kingston, Chisholm, arrived in Greenock from St Kitts with sugar, 23.7.1754.

#342   Elizabeth, Morrison, arrived in Greenock from Virginia with tobacco 22.7.1754.

#343   Friendship, Armour, arrived in Ayr from Virginia with tobacco, 6.8.1754.

#344   Port Glasgow, McClintock, arrived in Port Glasgow from Antigua with sugar and cotton; Caledonia, Warden, from Greenock to Boston with coal and balegoods; Augustus Caesar, Coutts, arrived in Aberdeen from Jamaica with rum; 8.1754.

Note that the Pressgang had taken the crew of the Falmouth of Glasgow in Virginia.

#345   Extract of a letter written on board the Catherine of Glasgow off Cape Henry, Virginia, 1.7.1754.

Kilmaurs, Boyd, arrived in Port Glasgow from Jamaica with sugar; Lilly, Somervell, arrived in Port Glasgow from Maryland with tobacco; Mally, Crawford, arrived in Greenock from Virginia with tobacco; and Hyndman, Lyon, arrived in Greenock from the West Indies with sugar, 8.1754.

Ronald McDonnel, found guilty of enlisting in French service, was banished to HM Plantations in America for 7 years, at Edinburgh 15.8.1754.

#347   Cary, Brown, Prince William, Donald, and Margaret, Gordon, all from Greenock to Virginia while the Crawford, Corry, sailed from Greenock to Boston, all with bale goods, 14.8.1754.

#348   Blackburn, Ewing, and Donald, Andrew, arrived in Greenock from Virginia with tobacco, 31.8.1754; Amity, Boyd, arrived in Ayr from Virginia with tobacco; and Isabella,

Simons, arrived in Leith from New York with wood 2.9.1754; while the Planter of Aberdeen, Ogilvie, sailed from Aberdeen to Jamaica.

#349 Joanna, Coulter, arrived in Greenock from Virginia with tobacco; Alexander and James, Wotherspoon, arrived in Greenock from the West Indies with sugar and cotton; Lilly, Somervell, from Greenock to Virginia with balegoods; Endeavour, Watson, from Leith to Carolina 10.9.1754; and the Fanny and Betty of Aberdeen, Thomson, arrived in Aberdeen from Virginia, 9.1754.

#350 Industry, Warden, arrived in Greenock from the West Indies 16.9.1754; Port Glasgow, McLintock, from Glasgow to Antigua with bale goods; Glasgow, Clerk, from Greenock to Virginia with bale goods; Cassandra, Hutchison, from Greenock to Philadelphia and Jamaica with bale goods, 9.1754.

William Stonyer, a grenadier in Wolfe's Regiment, Kenneth McDonald or McEannier, a farmer in Ross-shire, thieves, petitioned for transportation to America for life, which was granted, at Edinburgh 6.9.1754; while Margaret Rae, wife of George Chrystie in Echt, a thief, petitioned for banishment to America for life, which was granted, at Aberdeen 9.1754.

#351 William of Irvine, MacLean, arrived in Leith from Virginia with tobacco, and Industry, Cowan, from Leith to Carolina with merchant goods, 26.9.1754.

#352 Hawk, Heastie, arrived in Greenock from Virginia with pitch and tar, 8.10.1754.

#353 Caesar, Wyllie, arrived in Greenock from Jamaica with sugar, 10.10.1754; while Peggy, Boyer, Duke of Cumberland, Dunlop, Grizie, White, Dennistoun, Carnegie, and Cochrane, Semple, all arrived in Greenock from Virginia with tobacco; Queensberry of Dumfries, Bell, arrived in Leith from Virginia, 10.1754.

Letter from Virginia to a gentleman in Glasgow about the French settlements on the St Lawrence, along the Ohio, and in Mississippi.

#356 Nancy of Glasgow, Morrison, arrived in London from Boston 10.1754; Sally, Hyndman, from Greenock to St Kitts with balegoods 10.1754.

#357 Falmouth, Anderson, arrived in Port Glasgow from Virginia 11.1754; Adventure, James Hamilton, arrived in Leith from Jamaica with rum, sugar and cotton, 11.1754.

#358 Jean and Betty, Smith, arrived in Greenock from St Kitts with sugar 11.1754.

#359 Mattie, Orr, arrived in Greenock from Virginia with tobacco 17.11.1754; Neptune, Allan, arrived in Greenock from New York with pitch and tar 10.1754; Mally, Crawford, from Greenock via Cork to Barbados with tobacco and herring.

#360 Binning, Steel, from Greenock to Virginia with bale goods 30.11.1754.

#362 Murdoch, Hamilton, and Bogle, ..., arrived in Greenock from Virginia with tobacco 9.12.1754.

#363 Jeannie, Douglas, and Jean, How, arrived in Greenock from Virginia with tobacco 14.12.1754; United Janets, Anderson, arrived in Leith from New York with naval stores 16.12.1754.

#364 Caledonia, Warden, arrived in Glasgow from New England with oil and lintseed 23.12.1754.

#365 Mary, Fleming, and Peggy, Yuill, from Greenock via Cork to St Kitts, and Kingston, Chisholm, from Greenock to St Kitts both with herring 28.12.1754.

George Johnston and Andrew Mason, guilty of assault, were whipped through Edinburgh and Canongate, then imprisoned awaiting transportation to HM Plantations in America, 1.1.1755.

#366 Margaret, Gordon, arrived in Loch Ryan from Virginia with tobacco 10.1.1755; Alexander and James, Rowan, from Greenock to Barbados, Donald, Andrew, from Greenock to Virginia, and Caesar, Wyllie, from Greenock via Cork to Jamaica, all with bale goods, 5.1.1755.

#367 Margaret, Gordon, arrived in Greenock from Virginia with tobacco 1.1755.

#368 Dreghorn, Andrew, and Rebecca, Craig, arrived in Greenock from Virginia with tobacco 1.1755; Kilmaurs, Boyd, from Greenock to Jamaica with bale goods, and Susannah, Laing, from Greenock to Barbados with herring; Montrose, Moodie, and Hope, Moodie, arrived in Montrose from Virginia with tobacco and staves, 1.1755.

#369 Glasgow, Clark, Nelly, Galbraith, Brothers, Hunter, arrived in Greenock from Virginia with tobacco 23.1.1755;

Montrose of Montrose, Moodie, arrived in Aberdeen from Virginia with tobacco 1.1755.

"We have the agreeable accounts that the Planter of Aberdeen, Captain Ogilvie, who sailed from Cromarty 1st October last, arrived safe at Antigua 1st Decenber and though there were 80 people on board there was not any complaint of the slightest disposition among them." 4.2.1755.

#370   Katherine, Wyllie, from Greenock to South Carolina with bale goods, and Demmistoun, Carnegie, from Greenock to the West Indies with herring, 1.2.1755; Alexander and Anne, Hunter, from Aberdeen to Virginia 2.1755.

#371   Cary, Brown, and Pearl, Francis, arrived in Greenock from Virginia with tobacco, and Neptune, Weir, arrived in Greenock from Philadelphia with timber, 8.2.1755; Leith Galley, John Sharp, from Leith to Jamaica 9.2.1755; Hope of Aberdeen, Moodie, arrived in Aberdeen from Virginia with tobacco 2.1755.

#372   Arcturus, Brown, arrived in Leith from Philadelphia with flaxseed and pig-iron 20.2.1755.

#374   Jean and Elizabeth of Aberdeen, Walker, arrived in Aberdeen from Virginia with tobacco 3.1755.

#378   Lilly, Somervell, Betty, Chalmers, Jenny, McTaggart, arrived in Greenock from Virginia with tobacco 19.3.1755; Fanny and Betty of Aberdeen, Thomson, from Aberdeen to Virginia 4.1755.

#380   Homer, Hoggart, arrived in Greenock from Rhode Island with flaxseed and tar, 4.1755.

#382   Margaret, Gordon, Boyd, Douglas, Grizie, Dunlop, Rebecca, Craig, Jean, How, Cary, Brown, Andrew, Campbell, Menie, Tran, Bolling, Douglas, all from Greenock to Virginia with bale goods 5.1755; Mermaid, Campbell, from Greenock to Newfoundland, Hyndman, Lyon, from Greenock to St Kitts with herring, 5.1755.

"Advertisement. For Kingston, Jamaica, the Augustus Caesar, John Coutts commander, ... any young men, millwrights, joiners, masons, blacksmiths, labourers, and others who will engage themselves for 4 years shall meet with the greatest encouragement and be sure of good masters. In the captain's absence enquire of Mr John Leslie, merchant in Aberdeen." 6.5.1755.

Francis Porter, thief, and Patrick Aedie or McGregor, horse thief, both petitioned for banishment to America, which was granted, at Perth; Alexander Gall, sheep stealer, and Margaret Forbes, childmurderer, petitioned for banishment to America, which was granted, at Aberdeen, 5.1755.

#384   Jean and Betty, Smith, Greenock to St Kitts with herring and balegoods; Prince William, Donald, from Greenock to Virginia with balegoods 12.5.1755.

Carnten, McGee, arrived in Greenock from Barbados and New London with flaxseed and lumber; Greenock, McCunn, and Mary, Shannon, from Greenock to Virginia with balegoods.

#385   Grand Bank, Kelleren, arrived in Greenock from Boston with flaxseed and lumber; Beaufort, Kilburn, arrived in Greenock from St Kitts with sugar; and Binning, Steel, arrived in Greenock from Virginia with tobacco; Betty, Craig, from Greenock to the West Indies with herring; Joanna, Warden, from Greenock to Barbados via Cork with herring and tobacco; Bogle, Montgomery, and Dunlop, Boyle, from Greenock to Virginia with bale goods, 17.4.1755.

John McFarlane alias McAndrew in Skye, a sheepstealer, petitioned to be transported to America, which was granted at Inverness 17.5.1755.

#386   Blackburn, Ewing, and Boyd, Douglas, from Greenock to Virginia with balegoods 6.1755.

Industry of Leith, Cowan, at Stromness from Charleston, South Carolina, 20.5.1755.

Captain Archibald Grant married Miss Callendar, daughter of Dr Callendar deceased in Jamaica, at Monymusk 27.5.1755.

#388   Pearl, Francis, from Greenock to Virginia with balegoods 17.6.1755; Leathly of Aberdeen, Lickly, arrived in Aberdeen from Maryland with tobacco and staves, and Jean and Elizabeth of Aberdeen, Walker, and Hope of Montrose, Moody, sailed from Aberdeen to Virginia with merchant goods. 6.1755.

"On Saturday, Margaret Rae from the parish of Echt for cowstealing, banished at the October Circuit; Alexander Gall, from Peterhead, for sheep stealing, and Margaret Forbes, from Kirkton of Touch, for child murder, banished last Circuit, were put upon the Hope, Captain Moodie, bound for Virginia."

#389 Anne, Jamieson, from Greenock to Virginia, and Beaufort, Kelburn, from Greenock to St Kitts, both with merchant goods 16.6.1755.

#390 Brothers, Hunter, and Peggy, Boyd, from Greenock to Virginia with balegoods; St Mungo, Hall, from Greenock to Barbados with herring and balegoods, 21.6.1755.

#391 Cumberland, Dunlop, arrived in Greenock from Virginia with tobacco 29.6.1755; Cassandra, Hutchison, arrived in Greenock from Jamaica with rum and sugar 24.6.1755; and Binning, Steel, from Greenock to Virginia with balegoods 6.1755.

#392 Batchelor, Ewing, from Greenock to New England 15.7.1755. Letter dated 19.5.1755 from a gentleman in Philadelphia to his friend in Edinburgh discussing Braddock's expedition against the French.

#393 Friendship, Armour, arrived in Ayr from Virginia with tobacco; Montrose, Graham, arrived in Greenock from St Kitts with sugar; Eleanora, Wallace, arrived in Greenock from Barbados, 7.1755.

#394 Argyll, King, arrived in Greenock from Jamaica, and Kingdom, Chisholm, arrived in Greenock from St Kitts, both with sugar and rum 7.1755.

#395 Port Glasgow, McLintock, arrived in Greenock from Antigua with sugar and rum, 5.8.1755.

#396 Concord, arrived in Ayr from Virginia; Donald, Andrew, arrived in Greenock from Virginia with tobacco; Crawford, Corrie, from Greenock to Boston with balegoods; Betty, Morison, from Greenock to Virginia; and Wilmington, Murray, arrived in Leith from Jamaica with rum, mahogany, cotton and sugar, 8.1755.

#397 Kilmaurs, Boyd, arrived in Greenock from Jamaica with sugar, rum and cotton; Augustus Caesar, Coutts, from Aberdeen to Jamaica, 8.1755. Extract of a letter from Boston dated 14.6.1755 concerning the defence of the colonies.

#398 Eglinton, McTaggart, arrived in Greenock from Carolina, and Mermaid, Thom, arrived in Greenock from Boston with lumber, 8.1755.

#399   Mally, Crawford, and Margaret, Gordon, arrived in Greenock from Virginia with tobacco, after a 5 week crossing. 2.9.1755.

#400   Amity of Ayr, Boyd, arrived in Loch Ryan from Virginia, 9.1755.

Extract of a letter from Virginia concerning Braddock's campaign.

Janet Duncan, from Glen Isla in Angus, guilty of child-murder, was banished to HM Plantations in America for life, at Perth 9.1755.

#401   Caesar, Wyllie, arrived in Greenock from Jamaica with sugar and cotton 6.9.1755; Alexander and Anne of Aberdeen, Hunter, arrived in Aberdeen from Jamaica; Bachelor, Alexander, arrived in Greenock from Virginia with tobacco; Peggy, Yuill, arrived in Greenock from the West Indies with sugar and cotton, 9.1755.

Donald MacTavish and Donald MacKillcandrick, suspected murderers, petitioned for and were granted banishment to America, at Inverness 11.9.1755.

#403   Alexander and James, Rowand, arrived in Greenock from the West Indies; Anderson, Campbell, arrived in Rothesay from Virginia; and Royal Widow, Hutcheson, from Greenock to Jamaica with bale goods, 9.1755.

Extract from a letter from Port Royal, Virginia, to a gentleman in Glasgow concerning military affairs in America, dated 28.7.1755.

Gregor Roy McGregor alias Grant, accused of stealing 4 sheep, petitioned for and was granted banishment, at Aberdeen 9.1755.

#404   Alexander and James, Rowand, and Jean and Betty, Smith, arrived in Greenock from the West Indies with sugar and cotton; Anderson , Campbell, Bedford, Brown, and Judith, Sedgwick, arrived in Greenock from Virginia with tobacco. 27.9.1755.

#405   Caledonia, Warden, arrived in Greenock from Boston with oil and lumber 4.10.1755; Jean, Howe, and Dennistoun, Carnegie, arrived in Greenock from Virginia with tobacco; and Eglinton, Fisher, arrived in Greenock from Montserrat with sugar, 10.1755; America arrived in Ayr from Virginia in 6 weeks; and Industry, Cowan, from Leith to Carolina 7.10.1755.

Extracts of letters from Virginia and New England with news of the defeat on the Ohio.

#406 Susanna, Laing, and Industry, Warden, arrived in the Isle of Man from the West Indies; Grizie, Dunlop, and Jenny, Paterson, arrived in Greenock from Virginia with tobacco; Margaret, Gordon, from Greenock to Virginia; Fanny and Betty of Aberdeen, Thomson, arrived in Aberdeen from Virginia, 10.1755.

"Friday last, Gregor Roy MacGregor alias Grant who was banished by the Lords of Justiciary at their last Circuit Court here, was discharged from prison, being delivered over to a merchant of this place, in order to be transported to America."

#407 Rebecca, Craig, and Cary, Brown, arrived in Greenock from Virginia with tobacco 20.10.1755.

Mr Charles Gordon, a merchant in Jamaica, died there.

#409 Industry, Warden, arrived in Greenock from the West Indies with sugar and rum; Nancy, Crawford, from Greenock to Virginia and Nancy, Heastie, from Greenock to Boston, both with bale goods 11.1755.

Mr Alexander MacFarlane, brother of Walter MacFarlane of that Ilk, an eminent merchant in Jamaica, died there.

#410 Cochran, Sempill, and Adventure, Paterson arrived in Greenock from Virginia with tobacco 10.11.1755.

#411 Falmouth, Anderson, arrived in Greenock from Virginia with tobacco 15.11.1755; Robert, Watson, from Greenock to Virginia, and Dennistoun, Carnegie, from Greenock to Carolina, both with bale goods, 11.1755.

#412 Anne, Jamieson, Bolling, Douglas, and Prince William, Donald, arrived in Greenock from Virginia with tobacco 11.11.1755; Beaufort, Kelburn, arrived in Greenock from St Kitts with sugar.

#413 Gregor Roy McGregor alias Grant, was re-imprisoned as an opportunity to transport him to America had not been found.

#414 Eglinton, McAuslan, from Greenock to South Carolina with bale goods 12.1755.

#415 Dunlop, Bogle, and Binning, Steel, arrived in Greenock from Virginia with tobacco 18.12.1755; Hope of Aberdeen, Moodie, arrived in Aberdeen from Virginia with tobacco and staves, 12.1755.

#416	Elizabeth and Janet, Orr, arrived in Greenock from St Kitts with sugar, and Harwood, Dick, arrived in Greenock from Virginia with tobacco, 12.1755.
#417	Melietabell, Trail, arrived in Greenock from Boston with flaxseed and oil 27.12.1755; Nelly, Galbraith, and Bogle, Montgomerie, arrived in Greenock from Virginia, 12.1755.
#418	Charles, Glasford, arrived in Bo'ness from Virginia with tobacco; Brothers, Hunter, and Jean, Robertson, arrived in Greenock from Virginia with tobacco; Rebekah, Craig, from Greenock to South Carolina, and Elizabeth, Weir, from Greenock to Antigua, both with bale goods, 1.1756.
#419	Mary, Shannon, Blackburn, Ewing, and Pearl, Francis, arrived in Greenock from Virginia with tobacco 1.1756.
#420	Brothers, Andrew, arrived in Ayr, and Peggy, Boyd, arrived in Greenock, both from Virginia with tobacco, 1.1756.
#421	Dreghorn, Andrew, and Glasgow, Clark, both arrived in Greenock from Virginia with tobacco, 24.1.1756
#422	Crawford, Craig, arrived in Kirkcudbright from Boston ; Thistle, Murray, arrived in Leith from Virginia with tobacco; Christian, Watt, arrived in Leith from Maryland with lintseed and lumber, 2.1756
#425	Donald, Andrew, and Margaret, Gordon, arrived in Glasgow from Virginia with tobacco; Montrose, Walkingshaw, from Glasgow to Jamaica; Kingston, Chisholm, Sally, Hamilton, and Beaufort, Kelburn, from Glasgow to St Kitts; Anne, Jamieson, Brothers Adventure, Paterson, and Menie, Gemmel, to South Carolina; Suize, Morrison, to Virginia, Industry, Warden, to Antigua, all with bale goods and herring, 3.1756.
#426	Caesar, Wyllie, from Greenock to Jamaica, Beaufort, Kelburn, from Greenock to St Kitts, and Port Glasgow, Reid, from Greenock to Antigua, 28.2.1756
#427	John Ogilvie of Quoich to be transported for life 3.1756
#428	Two Sisters, Pinkerton, from Greenock to the Isle of May and Barbados with merchant goods; Port Glasgow, Reid, from Greenock to Antigua with herring, 3.1756
#430	Extract of a letter from Jamaica dated 15.12.1755. "Gregor Roy MacGregor alias Grant, banished last Circuit Court, was shipped for Virginia."

Fanny and Betty of Aberdeen, Thomson, from Aberdeen to
Virginia with sail cloth; Leathly of Aberdeen, Lickly, from
Aberdeen to Virginia with merchant goods, 4.1756

#431 "We hear from Barra, that a large ship from Philadelphia for
Ireland loaded with lintseed and iron bars was lately cast
away there, 18 passengers and sailors who took to the
long-boat perished, the master and 4 hands who stayed
by the ship are saved. This is the third wreck this
season of ships from Philadelphia for Ireland amongst
the Western Isles." 8.4.1756

"The recruits for Lord John Murray's Regiment of Scots
Highlanders are to be transported directly from the
Clyde for North America." 4.1756

#433 'Last week the Bolling, Douglas, Nelly, Galbraith, Philadephia,
Fergusson, and Jenny, Motherwell, were taken to
transport troops from the Clyde to New York.' 4.1756.

Excedo, Acton, arrived in Greenock from Maryland with
flaxseed; Mermaid, Campbell, from Greenock via Cork
to Newfoundland with tobacco and herring; Anderson,
Campbell, and Donald, Andrew, from Greenock to
Virginia with balegoods, 17.4.1756.

#434 Catherine, Wyllie, arrived in Greenock from Maryland with
tobacco; Nancy, Heastie, arrived in Greenock from
Boston with hides and flaxseed; Dunlop, Boyle, from
Greenock to South Carolina, Pearl, Francis, from
Greenock to Virginia, and Glasgow, Clark, from
Greenock to Virginia, all with bale goods; Friendship,
Lyon from Greenock via Cork to St Kitts with herring,
24.4.1756. Britannia of Greenock, Thomson, at
Stromness on way to Leith from Virginia 4.1756, and
Jean and Elizabeth of Aberdeen, Walker, arrived in
Aberdeen from Virginia with tobacco, 4.1756.

#435 Alexander, Hamilton, arrived in Leith from Maryland and
Virginia with flaxseed, planks and staves, 4.5.1756.

Jean Steven, accused of childmurder, petitoned for and was
granted banishment to America, as were Elizabeth
Smith and Margaret Grant or McIntosh, alleged thieves,
at Aberdeen 5.1756.

"At one o'clock came to town {Aberdeen}, escorted by an
Officer's Command of the Cameronian Regiment from
Inverness, 34 impressed men from that county to join

Lord Loudon's Regiment now destined for the American Service."

#436   Margaret, Gordon, and Lilly, White, from Greenock to Virginia with balegoods; and Hawk, Campbell from Greenock via Cork to Jamaica and Jean and Betty, Smith, from Greenock via Cork to St Kitts both with herring 8.5.1756.

#437   Nancy, Crawford, arrived in Greenock from Virginia with tobacco, and Betty, Watson, from Greenock to Antigua with herring 8.5.1756.

#439   Tibby, Paterson, from Greenock via Cork to Barbados with balegoods 29.5.1756; Forth, Brown, from Leith to Virginia 5.1756.

#440   America of Rhode Island, Jefferson, at Stromness on way to Amsterdam 26.5.1756.

#441   Lilly, Somervell, arrived in Greenock from Virginia with tobacco 11.6.1756; Rekie of Aberdeen, Salmon, arrived in Aberdeen from Jamaica with sugar, wine and logwood.

#442   Robert, Watson, and Concord, Orr, arrived in Greenock from Virginia with tar and tobacco; Aschah, Hayward, from Greenock to Maryland with balegoods, 6.1756.

#443   Kilmaurs, Graham, arrived in Greenock from St Kitts and Port Glasgow, Haddington. arrived in Greenock from Antigua, both with sugar and cotton; Brothers, Hunter, from Greenock to Virginia with balegoods, 7.1756.

"Yesterday arrived in the Road of Leith on her voyage to London, Devonshire, Captain Jacobson, in 6 weeks from Boston, New England, ..." 29.6.1756.

#444   John and Mary of Peterhead, Arbuthnott, arrived at Hoyhead, Orkney, from Virginia, for London, 7.1756.

#445   Royal Widow, Hutcheson, arrived in Greenock from Jamaica with sugar and rum, 20.7.1756; Catherine, Thomson, from Greenock to Virginia with balegoods.

#446   Susie, Morrison, arrived in Greenock from Virginia with tobacco, and Industry, Bruce, arrived in Greenock from Jamaica with sugar 8.7.1756

Letter from Virginia re the war in America.

#447   Anne, Jamieson, arrived in Bo'ness from South Carolina with rice 3.8.1756.

#448   Severn, Wilson, arrived in Greenock from Jamaica with sugar and rum; Bedford, Brown, from Greenock to Virginia with balegoods, 8.1756.

#449   Rebecca, Craig, arrived in Greenock from South Carolina with rice and Cary, Brown, arrived in Greenock from Virginia with tobacco, 7.8.1756; Lilly, Somervill, Prince William, Orr, and Concord, Moodie, from Greenock to Virginia with balegoods.

#450   Grizie, Dunlop, arrived in Greenock from Virginia with tobacco, and Kingston, Chisholm, arrived in Greenock from St Kitts with sugar and cotton, 14.8.1756.

"On Friday Elizabeth Smith, Jean Steven and Margaret Grant, were put on board the St Andrew, Captain Dunbar, for Virginia, conform to the sentence of the last Circuit." 20.8.1756.

#451   Alexander and James, Rowan, from Antigua and Beaufort, Kelburn, from St Kitts, arrived in Greenock with sugar and cotton 31.8.1756.

#452   Anderson, Campbell, arrived in Loch Ryan, and Betty, Morrison, arrived in Greenock both from Virginia with tobacco 8.9.1757. Brilliant of New York, Jefferson, at Stromness from Amsterdam; Sally of London, Dick, at Stromness from Virginia; Polly of Rhode Island, Boardman, at Stromness for Amsterdam, 18.8.1756.

Extract of a letter brought from the James River, Virginia, to the Clyde on the Donald, master John Andrew, in 29 days.

#453   Grand Bank, Starret, arrived in the Clyde from Barbados 6.9.1756. Anderson, Campbell, Little Mally, Crawford, Donald, Andrew, and Margaret, Gordon, arrived in Greenock from Virginia with tobacco 9.1756. Port Glasgow, Reid, from Antigua, and Sally, Hamilton,from St Kitts, both arrived in Greenock with sugar; Caledonia, Watson, arrived in Greenock from Boston with oil, 9.1756.

Extract of a letter from Boston dated 26 July re French and Indian War; and a letter from the camp at Fort Hardy dated 18.7.1756.

John Grant or Bittack, housebreaker, petitioned for and was granted banishment to America for life, at Inverness 9.1756. Alexander Cumming, thief, petitioned for and

was granted banishment to America for life, at
Aberdeen 9.1756.

#454 Jean and Betty, Smith, Industry, Mure, and Elizabeth,
Morrison, arrived in Greenock from St Kitts with sugar
21.9.1756. Blackburn, Ewing, and Jean, Howe, from
Greenock to Virginia. Dennistoun, Carnegie, from
Greenock via Cork to the West Indies with bale goods

#456 Cary, Brown, from Greenock to Virginia, Peggy, Buchanan,
and Nancy, Hamilton, from Greenock to South
Carolina, all with bale goods 5.10.1756.

#457 Caesar, Wyllie, Montrose, Walkingshaw, Jenny, McTaggart,
and Hawke, Campbell, arrived in Greenock from
Jamaica with sugar, rum and cotton. Binning,
Colquhoun, arrived in   Greenock from Virginia with
tobacco. Royal Widow, Hutchison, from Greenock to
Philadelphia and Jamaica, and the Betty, Morrison, from
Greenock to Virginia, both with bale goods, 10.1756.

#460 Alexander and James, Rowan, from Greenock to St Kitts with
balegoods 23.10.1756; Wilmington of Leith, Murray,
arrived at Stromness from Jamaica 5.10.1756; Helen of
Leith, and Edinburgh of Leith, ..., at Stromness on way
to South Carolina, 10.1756.

#461 Letter from Montserrat dated 31.8.1756 re use of Dutch
passes by French vessels.
Extract of a letter from Boston to Glasgow re capture of
Oswego.

#462 Murdoch, Hamilton, and Glasgow, Clark, arrived in Greenock
from Virginia with tobacco 23.10.1756; Loudon, King,
arrived in Greenock from Boston with pitch and tar.

#463 Menie, Gemmell, arrived in Greenock from South Carolina
with rice; Cochran, Sempill, arived in Greenock from
Virginia with tobacco; Isabella, Hyndman, from
Greenock to St Kitts via Cork; Boyd. Fleming, and
Susie, Morison, from Greenock to Virginia; Fanny and
Betty of Aberdeen, Thomson, arrived in Orkney from
Virginia with tobacco.
"This morning [18.11.1756] William Stevenson of Dykes
sentenced by the Lords of Justiciary for forgery, and
John Ogilvie of Quoich, for an intention to murder,
together with Janet Tass and her daughter, for theft,
were sent [from Edinburgh] to Leith under a guard in
order to be transported to America"

#466	Hawk, Campbell, and Falmouth, Robertson, arrived in Greenock from the West Indies with sugar and rum; Pearl, Francis, arrived in Greenock from Virginia with tobacco; Peggie, Buchanan, from Greenock to South Carolina with balegoods; and Elizabeth, Dick, from Greenock to Barbados with herring, 14.12.1756.
#467	America, Francis, and Brothers, Hunter, arrived in Greenock from Virginia with tobacco; and Mary, Hyndman, arrived in Greenock from Virginia with tobacco and pitch, 11.12.1756.
#468	Leathly of Aberdeen, Lickly, arrived in Aberdeen from Virginia with tobacco, 28.12.1756.
#470	Margaret, Gordon, from Greenock to Virginia with bale goods; Susannah, Ewing, from Greenock via Cork to Antigua, Loudon, Cuddie, from Greenock via Cork to St Kitts, and Dreghorn, Kelburn, from Greenock to Jamaica, all with herring, 3.1.1757. Fanny and Betty of Aberdeen, Thomson, at Stromness from Virginia for Aberdeen, and Charles of Bo'ness, Glasford, at Stromness from Virginia for Bo'ness, both with tobacco 1.1757.
#471	Lilly, White, arrived in Greenock from Virginia with tobacco; Industry, Mure, and Mally, Tucker, both from Greenock to Virginia, and Kingston, Chisholm, from Greenock to St Kitts, all with bale goods, 8.1.1757.
#473	Nelly, Galbreath, Catherine, Thomson, and Jenny, Tran, arrived in Greenock from Virginia with tobacco, 22.1.1757.
#474	Anderson, Campbell, and Glasgow, Coats, from Greenock to Virginia with bale goods; Hawke, Campbell, from Greenock to Jamaica with herring, 1.1757.
#475	Bedford, Brown, and Tibby, Paterson, arrived in Greenock from Virginia with tobacco 6.2.1757.
#480	Extract of a letter from Petersburgh, on the Appomattox River, Virginia, dated 3.2.1757 to Aberdeen with news of military affairs there.
	Report of two battalions of Highlanders about to embark for America, 3.1757.
#482	St Andrew of Aberdeen, Dunbar, arrived in Aberdeen from Virginia with tobacco and staves, and the Delaware, Captain Rag, put into Aberdeen on way from Philadelphia to Leith, 12.4.1757.

#483	Alexander Cumming, a blacksmith, banished at the last Circuit court, and two young women, for petty theft, were put upon the Montrose in order for transportation, 12.4.1757. Montrose of Aberdeen, Greig, from Aberdeen to Virginia 4.1757.
#490	Margaret of Glasgow, Gordon, arrived in Greenock from Virginia in 30 days, bringing news of events at Fort Edward involving Highland troops, 26.5.1757. Jean Hendry, from Forfar, accused of child murder, petitioned for and was granted transportation to America, at Perth 21.5.1757.
#492	Glassford, Hume, arrived at Loch Ryan from South Carolina with rice 6.6.1757.
#497	Granville, Fennel, arrived in Greenock from North Carolina with 5000 bushels of Indian corn, 12.7.1757.
#499	Jeannie of London, Crawford, at Stromness 12.7.1757, en route from Virginia to London; Christian of Leith, George Watt, arrived in Liverpool from Virginia 7.1757.
#501	St George of London, Moodie, at Stromness en route from Virginia to London 18.7.1757; Hair of Rhode Island, Banker, at Stromness on way from Rhode Island to Hamburg 20.7.1757; Jevon of New York, Hysham, at Stromness 25.7.1757 on way from Hamburg to New York; Prince Frederick, Trattles, at Stromness from North Carolina on way to Hull 16.7.1757.
#502	Charming Nancy of New York, Munds, at Stromness on way from New York to Amsterdam 1.8.1757.
#503	Cathcart, arrived in Greenock from Virginia 30.8.1757.
#505	Alexander Findlay, from Forfar, a fireraiser, petitioned for and was granted banishment, at Perth 9.1757.
#506	Pomona, Smith, from Rhode Island, and Hannibal of New York, Bryson, at Stromness on way to Amsterdam 24.8.1757.
#507	Margaret Grant, indicted of wilfull fireraising, petitioned and was granted banishment to America for life, at Aberdeen 9.1757.
#514	Pearl, Francis, and Trial, Crawford, arrived in the Clyde from Virginia 15.11.1757.
#515	Extract of a letter from Boston, dated 5.9.1757, re naval and military activities in America.

Charles, Glasford, arrived in Burntisland from Virginia
11.1757; Bedford, Clark, arrived in Loch Ryan from
Virginia; Achilles, Noble, arrived in Greenock from
Boston with pitch and tar 12.11.1757; Tibby,
Archdeacon, from Greenock to the West Indies with
herring.

#516   Greenock, McCunn, Charming Nancy, Montgomerie, Prince
William, Orr, Jenny, Rayburn, Bedford, Clark, Mary, and
Scott, Dutchess, Young, arrived in Greenock from
Virginia with tobacco 29.11.1757. Dreghorn, Kelburn,
Hawk, Campbell, and Montrose, Walkingshaw, arrived
in Greenock from Jamaica with sugar, and Finlay,
Coulter, arrived in Greenock from Barbados with sugar
and rum, 11.1757.

#519   Extract from a letter from an officer of Montgomerie's
Highlanders in South Carolina dated 17.9.1757.
Murdoch, McCunn, from Greenock to Virginia with merchant
goods 10.12.1757.

#528   Lilly, White, Earl of Loudoun, Tabbe, and Betty, Heastie,
arrived in Greenock from Virginia with tobacco, while
Pretty Jenny, Kirkwood, arrived in Greenock from
Jamaica with rum and sugar, 8.2.1758.

529   Isabella, Chisholm, Alexander and James, Rowan, from
Greenock to St Kitts, while Gordon, King, from
Greenock to Antigua, all with balegoods and herring;
while Jenny, Hyndman, from Greenock to Virginia with
balegoods, 2.1758. Rebecca, Hamilton, arrived at the
Sound of Islay from South Carolina 2.1758. Matty of
Dunbar, Middlemiss, at Stromness on way from South
Carolina to Dunbar 1.2.1758.

530   Rebecca, Hamilton, arrived in Greenock from South Carolina
with rice, and Friendship, Morrison, arrived in Greenock
from Virginia with tobacco, 9.2.1758. Prince William,
Orr, and Margaret, Robertson, from Greenock to
Virginia with balegoods, 2.1758.

531   "Last week came from Perth under a strong guard, 2 women
and 4 men under sentence of transportation to be
shipped at the first opportunity." 14.3.1758.

533   "On Thursday last Angus Stuart banished at the last Circuit
Court for theft, and Margaret Grant banished at the

	same time for wilful fire raising, and likewise 6 criminals from Perth were shipped off for Virginia according to their sentence." 3.1758.
# 533	Montrose of Aberdeen, Greig, and Leathly of Aberdeen, Lickly, from Aberdeen to Virginia 3.1758.
# 534	Matty of Leith, Captain Middlemiss, from Leith to South Carolina, sailed from Stromness 11.3.1758.
# 535	"For Kingston in Jamaica from the port of Aberdeen, the snow St Andrew, 150 tons burthen, master Arthur Gibbon, will good accommodation for passengers will sail against 1 May next .... any blacksmiths, joiners, millwrights, tailors or other articifers who are willing to indent for 4 years will meet with good encouragement. They may depend to be engaged to good masters who will use them well during their indentures and when the 4 years are expired they will be at liberty to do business for themselves and in a very short time may gain as much as enable them to live easily and comfortably. Such may apply to William Brebner and Company." 11.4.1758.
# 536	Success of Peterhead, Cordiner, at Stromness on way to Virginia, 29.3.1758, sailed from there 30.3.1758.
# 540	John MacNaughton, sometime in Glenlyon, indicted for theft, petitioned for banishment to America - which was granted, and Isabel Mortimer, indicted of child murder, petitioned for banishment to America - also granted, at Perth 5.1758.
# 541	Ochiltree arrived in the Clyde from Virginia, 5.1758.
# 542	St Andrew of Aberdeen, Gibbons, from Aberdeen to Jamaica 6.1758.
#549	Lists of troops engaged in the attacks on Louisbourg, Fort Du Chesne, Ticonderoga and Crown Point, including the Royal Scots, Fraser's Highlanders, Lord John Murray's 42nd Highlanders, and Colonel Montgomery's Highlanders.
#551	James Forbes, schoolmaster of a charity workhouse in Dalkeith, guilty of debauchery, sentenced to be whipped through Edinburgh and Dalkeith, and then banished to the Plantations for life, at Edinburgh 7.1758.
#557	Alexander Barclay, late a soldier of General Holmes' Regiment, guilty of robbery, was banished to the Plantations for life, at Edinburgh 9.1758.

Alexander Wanless, from Fife, guilty of theft from a
bleachfield, petitioned for and was granted banishment
to America, at Perth 9.1758.

#558   At the Orkneys in 4 weeks from Virginia the Montrose of
Aberdeen, Greg, for Aberdeen with tobacco 9.1758.

#559   James Hamilton, a tanner in Aberdeen, accused of stealing
skins, petitioned for and was granted banishment to the
Plantations for life, at Aberdeen 9.1758.

#560   "17 transports have been ordered to the Clyde to carry to
America the new raised company of the Royal Regiment
of Highlanders."

Montrose of Aberdeen, Greig, arrived in Aberdeen from
Virginia with tobacco.

#561   Marion Stevenson, guilty of stealing cloth from a bleachfield,
was banished to America for 7 years, at Ayr 23.9.1758.

#562   Extract of a letter from Winchester, Virginia, dated 6.8.1758 re
troop movements and a proposed attack on the Ohio.

#564   Reference to Mr Robert McPherson, chaplain to Colonel
Fraser's Regiment in America.

#565   "Wanted 2 young men, the one a brickmaker and the other a
country carpenter who understands the family business
of a milnwright - to engage to go to Jamaica and indent
for 4 years. Let them apply to the publisher of this paper
who will give them proper encouragement." 7.11.1758.

"For Boston in New England and New York. The brigantine
the Lovely Jean of Aberdeen, Captain John Leslie, of
about 120 tons burthen, mounting 4 carriage guns and 6
swivels, sails from hence by 25th inst. at furthest and
takes in goods upon freight at £3 per ton. She has good
accommodation for passengers, therefore all such as
shall intend to take their passage by her, may depend
on meeting with the best of usage and entertainment
and on the same terms as is paid from Leith or
Glasgow. For particulars enquire of David Shaw of this
place who will give good encouragement to articifers of
different kinds and stout lads who incline to the sea, and
will indent for 3 or 4 years; likewise to a qualified farmer,
well recommended, for the above place. Such whom
these proposals may suit are desired also to apply to Mr
John Shaw of Inverness and baillie John Duff of Elgin."
7.11.1758.

#567   Report on the aftermath of the Siege of Louisbourg.

#571 Lilly, Montgomerie, arrived in Greenock from Virginia with tobacco; Jean and Betty, Smith, and Beaufort, Golkison, from Greenock to St Kitts; Jeany, Hyndman, from Greenock to South Carolina with bale goods; Leathly of Aberdeen, Lickly, arrived in Aberdeen from Virginia with tobacco; 9.12.1758.

#572 Extract of a letter from Virginia re the Siege of Fort Du Quesne, 14.9.1758.

Duncan, Bogle, Christian, Montgomery, and Dolphin, Giller, arrived in Greenock from Virginia with tobacco; Lilly, arrived in Greenock from North Carolina with tar; Jean, Wilson, from Greenock to St Kitts with bale goods; Alexander of Leith, Moodie, at Stromness on way from North Carolina to Leith, and Mally, Watson, at Stromness on way from South Carolina to Leith, 12.1758.

#573 Nelly, Kerr, with lumber, and Susie, Peter, with tobacco, arrived in Greenock from Virginia; St Andrew, ..., arrived in Greenock from Jamaica with sugar, rum and cotton; Achilles, Graham, Isabella, Chisholm, Laurel, Laing, and Three Sisters, Laing, from Greenock to St Kitts, and Shannon, Orr, from Greenock to Barbados, all with bale goods; 13.12.1758. Hope, arrived in Lochindaal from Jamaica.

#575 Brothers, Anderson, Elizabeth, Robertson, Albany, Crawford, and Blackburn, Knible, arrived in Greenock from Virginia with tobacco and lumber; William, Noble, and Glendoick, Campbell, arrived in Greenock from North Carolina with pitch and tar; Kingston, Kelburn, and Hope, Hutchison, arrived in Greenock from Jamaica with sugar; Hawk, Campbell, to Jamaica, Jean, How, and Trial, Crawford, to Virginia, and Mally, Langmuir, to St Kitts, all from Greenock with bale goods.

#576 Montrose, Greig, from Aberdeen to Antigua with goods and passengers, 1.1759.

"Wanted to go to Jamaica to indent for 4 years - 2 housecarpenters and joiners, 1 brickmaker, 2 plowmen. Any person willing to engage may apply to John Ross, merchant in Aberdeen, who will give them encouragement."

#577 Lord Howe, Handy, arrived in Kirkwall from South Carolina, 1.1759.

#578	Charming Janet of Leith, Brown, arrived at Peterhead from Virginia with tobacco for Leith, 2.1759.
#581	Matty, Knox, Peggie, Morrison, and Bedford, Clark, from Greenock to Virginia with bale goods; Kingston, Williamson, for Antigua, Cathcart, Smith, and Montrose, Walkingshaw, for Jamaica, all from Greenock with herring, 2.1759.
#582	Nancy, Brown, and Rebecca, Ryburn, from Greenock to South Carolina; Cochran, Ewing, Buchanan, Morrison, and Grizel, Dunlop, all from Greenock to Virginia with bale goods, 24.2.1759. Lovely Jean of Aberdeen, from Aberdeen to Boston, New England, 3.1759.
#583	America, Gemmell, arrived in Greenock from Virginia with tobacco 3.3.1759.
#585	Marischal Keith, Gibson, arrived in Greenock from Philadelphia with flax seed, 17.3.1759; Dolly, Laing, arrived in Greenock from North Carolina with tar; Ingram, Ritchie, and Henderson, Hamilton, arrived in Greenock from Virginia with tobacco, 3.1759.
	Extract of a letter from Pittsburgh [formerly Fort Du Chesne] dated 2.1.1759 to a gentleman in Aberdeen stating that General Forbes had appointed Captain Alexander McKenzie of Balmoir, of Montgomery's Highlanders, as Governor of the Fort.
#586	Montrose of Aberdeen, Greig, from Aberdeen to Antigua.
#587	Porpus, Woodhouse, Lively, Shaftoe, and John's Endeavour, Weir, from Greenock to New York with Highlanders. King of Prussia, Baird, Janet and Mally, Ferguson, and Industry, Wilson, all to the West Indies, Eglinton, Buchanan, and Betsey, Anderson, both to Virginia, all from Greenock with bale goods, 4.1759. Peggy and Mally, Hoggart, arrived in Greenock from Boston with flax seed. Lovely Jean of Aberdeen, Leslie, from Stromness to Boston 14.3.1759.
#589	Prince William, Orr, and Margaret, Robertson, from Greenock to Virginia; Elizabeth, Robertson, from Greenock to Antigua; Susie, Gillespie, from Greenock to Boston, and William, Noble, to Philadelphia, all with bale goods 14.4.1759.
#590	Fanny and Betty of Aberdeen, Thomson, at Stromness from Virginia for London 5.1759.

#593   Extract of a letter from St Kitts dated 2.3.1759 re the sugar
price. Monro, Glasford, arrived in Greenock from
Carolina with rice, and Marischal Keith, Gibson, from
Greenock to Virginia with bale goods 14.5.1759; Tibby,
Archdeacon, Diamond, Gray, Betty, Warden, and
Jeannie, Omay, arrived from Virginia with tobacco.

Peter Grant alias Moir, Banffshire, acused of the theft of a
mare, was banished to America for 7 years at Aberdeen
26.5.1759. {He later enlisted in a Highland Regiment}

Extract of a letter from Captain Colin Douglas of the Betty,
who sailed from the Clyde to Jamaica, dated St Kitts
10.4.1759.

#610   "Wanted. About 12 or 15 good tradesmen namely joiners,
coopers, blacksmiths, etc., to go as 4 year servants to
the West Indies. They may depend on civil usage and
of having good masters provided for them as well as
good encouragement of yearly wages by applying to
Robert Forrest at Fraserburgh and also have monthly
pay from the time they enter on board the ship whereof
the said Robert Forrest goes master for doing what
duty they can till their arrival in the West Indies. NB
Such as are willing must apply before the 1st November
next and none will be accepted without a good
character." 18.9.1759.

#611   Erskine of Alloa, Nicol, arrived in Aberdeen from St Kitts with
rum.

John Wattie, in the parish of Towie, indicted for the murder of
James Stuart, petitioned for and was granted
banishment, at Aberdeen 9.1759.

#612   Dr Andrew Cassie, physician in St Katherine's parish,
Jamaica, bequethed a legacy to Aberdeen Infirmary,
9.1759.

#613   "Lately at St Croix in America one Jean Brown, a native of
Aberdeen or somewhere thereabouts, who went from
thence first to Philadelphia, afterwards to Barbados, and
from thence to St Croix and married to one Aspinall a
carpenter, who is likewise lately dead - whoever can
prove themselves her relations may be put in a way of
recovering her effects by applying to the publisher of this
paper." 16.10.1759.

#615   Item re the surrender of Quebec 18.9.1759 including lists of
killed or wounded officers of Fraser's Highlanders.

#616   Letter from an officer of Colonel Fraser's Regiment dated Quebec 20.9.1759 listing officers killed and wounded.

#619   Lovely Jean of Aberdeen, at Stromness on way from Halifax to Hamburg with sugar 11.1759.

#622   James of London, Simson, arrived in Aberdeen from Virginia with tobacco, and Helen of Aberdeen, Walker, arrived in Aberdeen from New York for Hamburg with sugar, 12.1759.

#623   Captain Simon Fraser of Colonel Fraser's Regiment, second son of Charles Fraser of Inveralochy, died at Quebec 15.10.1759 of wounds received 13.10.1759.

"For Virginia the Montrose, Archibald Greig commander, will sail 12 January 1760. There is excellent accommodation for passengers and any men, women or boys who incline an indenture may apply to the captain." 18.12.1759.

#628   "On Friday John Wattie, late farmer in the Parish of Towie, was shipt for Virginia conform to sentence of last circuit."

Montrose of Aberdeen, Greig, from Aberdeen to Virginia, 1.1760.

#658   Major Hardy, Cooper, and Montrose of Aberdeen, Greig, arrived in Aberdeen from Virginia bound for London with tobacco 8.1760.

#664   Agnes Baxter, accused of childmurder, petitioned for and was granted banishment to HM Plantations, at Perth 9.1760.

#665   The privateer Mars, James Weir, from Port Glasgow to St Kitts and Guadaloupe with passengers 6.10.1760.

#673   James, Simson, arrived in Aberdeen from Virginia with tobacco 12.1760.

#680   Unity of Aberdeen, Peter Thomson, bound for Halifax, was captured by a French privateer and carried to St Malo

Montrose of Aberdeen, Greig, from Aberdeen to Virginia.

#681   "For Kingston, Jamaica. The snow Jupiter of Aberdeen, Arthur Gibbon master, and will certainly sail before or after the 25 February next, with or without a convoy. For freight or passage, apply to the said commander who will serve them on the same terms as from London, Glasgow or Leith. If any tradesmen, such as smiths, housecarpenters, bricklayers, millwrights, coopers, who cannot pay their passage chuse to indent for a term of

years will apply to Captain Gibbon they will have all
due encouragement." 26.1.1761.

#687 "Wanted a house carpenter, well recommended, to go to
Jamaica and engage with a gentleman in that island for
the space of 4 years. Great encouragement will be
given. For particulars apply to the publisher of this
paper " 9.3.1761

#690 Jupiter of Aberdeen, Gibbon, from Aberdeen to Jamaica
30.4.1761.

#691 The brigantine Polly, Thomas Stonehouse, arrived in
Peterhead 4.5.1761 from Cape Fear, North Carolina,
bound for Whitby.

#704 Betty, Cathcart, arrived in Stromness from South Carolina
bound for Hamburg, and Britannia, Freeman, arrived in
Stromness from Boston bound for Amsterdam, 6.1761.

#705 Montrose of Aberdeen, Greig, arrived in Aberdeen from
Virginia bound for London 7.1761.

#708 Alexander Keir, a thief, was banished to the Plantations for
life, at Edinburgh 8.1761.

#710 John Clerk, 22, a merchant in Halifax, Nova Scotia, died in
Roxburgh near Boston, New England, 19.5.1761.

#715 William Tower, master of the snow Molly of Glasgow, was
captured on 17 August by Jean Francis Coke, master of
the privateer Romaine of Dunkirk, on passage from St
Croix to the Isle of Man.

#726 Extract of a letter from New York to a merchant in Glasgow re
military affairs 7.10.1761.

#741 Reverend William Proctor, born in Banff or Elgin, educated at
Aberdeen College, died in Nottoway parish, Virginia,
1761.

#748 Nelly of Aberdeen, Hervie, arrived in Aberdeen from North
Carolina 5.1762

#768 John McIntyre, a soldier in General Campbell's Regiment, a
thief, was banished to America for 14 years, at
Aberdeen 9.1762.

#770 Sally, David Ross, from Leith to Havanna with merchant
goods, 12.10.1762.

#771 Report concerning the capture of Newfoundland, 18.10.1762

#785 Betty Greig, Captain Watt, from Archangel to New York with a
cargo of hemp, iron, tallow and candles, was wrecked
on Cairnton Rock, Stromness, Orkney, 29.11.1762.

Harrison, Captain Duncan, arrived in Aberdeen from Virginia
7.3.1763.

#798 Edinburgh, 18.4.1763. "it is said that there are now only 6 of
the original soldiers left, of Lord John Murray's Highland
Regiment, who sailed from Britain to America, at the
beginning of the late war."

#807 Boyd, Captain Dunlop, arrived in Aberdeen from Virginia with
tobacco, 27.6.1763.

#812 Katherine, Captain Lawrence, from South Carolina sailed from
Stromness to Amsterdam 4.7.1763.

Little David, from New York, and Swift, Captain Fraser, from
Boston, sailed from Stromness to Newcastle 12.7.1763.

Charming Sally, Captain Taylor, from Hamburg, sailed from
Stromness to New York 14.7.1763.

Pitt, Captain Auld, from the Grenades, at Stromness on way
to Hamburg 16.7.1763.

#817 "Any wrights, coopers or smiths who are willing to engage to
serve in the way of their business for 4 or more years in
the island of Grenada [one of the most healthful places
in the West Indies] may apply to George Moir of
Scotstown at Aberdeen; or Messrs Arbuthnott and
Guthrie, merchants in Edinburgh, who will give them
suitable encouragement." 5.9.1763.

#818 Elizabeth Campbell, a soldier's wife and a pickpocket, was
banished to the Plantations for 7 years, at Ayr 1.9.1763.

#819 Helen Fraser, guilty of child murder, was banished to the
Plantations for life, at Aberdeen 1.9.1763.

James Collie, a horsehirer in Aberdeen, found guilty of assault
and attempted rape, was whipped through Aberdeen
then banished to America for life, at Aberdeen
1.9.1763.

#820 Alexander Schaw, a cattle thief, was banished to the
Plantations for 14 years, at Inverness 9.1763.

#826 "Wanted for Jamaica. Any well recommended young
tradesmen such as coppersmiths, blacksmiths,
millwrights, housecarpenters, masons and bricklayers,
who will engage for 4 years, may upon applying to
Alexander Dyce jr., merchant in Aberdeen, meet with
every good encouragement as they are wanted
immediately, and only a few; they must
understand country business and figures a little and will
engage for the aforesaid number of years, may upon

	application meet with suitable encouragement."
	7.11.1763.
#827	William Simpson Esquire, formerly an eminent .... in Edinburgh, is appointed Chief Justice of Georgia, with a salary of £500 per annum. ..... Simpson, son of the above is appointed Clerk of the Council of South Carolina, a place worth £350 per annum. James Moultrie is appointed Chief Justice of East Florida. 14.11.1763.
#829	"Wanted. Several tradesmen, viz. housecarpenters, millwrights, coopers, bricklayers and taylors to serve in Jamaica for 4 years. Those who are interested a little farming and day laborers will likewise be engaged. Any who are willing to engage may apply to John Burnett jr., merchant in Aberdeen, who will give them very good encouragement and they may depend on being well used abroad. The vessel goes from Leith and these who intend to go need apply soon as she will sail in a few weeks." 28.11.1763.
#833	Harrison, Captain Duncan, arrived in Aberdeen from Virginia 1.1764.
#836	Diamond, Captain Boyd, arrived in the Clyde from Virginia with tobacco 12.1763.
#846	Harrison, Captain Duncan, from Aberdeen to Virginia 3.1764.
#854	James Shearer, a barber in Ayr, guilty of rape, banished to the Plantations for 14 years, at Ayr 3.5.1764. Jean Laing, wife of Andrew Meiklehose a weaver in Walneuk of Paisley, a thief, banished to the Plantations for 14 years, at Glasgow 5.1764.
#855	John McNeil, a cattle thief, banished to the Plantations for 14 years, at Inveraray 5.1764.
#856	William Stephen, a student of divinity, guilty of fireraising, banished to the Plantations, at Stirling 5.1764.
#862	John Mackintosh, a sailor in Leith, guilty of housebreaking, banished to the Plantations for life, at Edinburgh 9.7.1764.
#863	John Barnet, servant to John Innes of Muiryfold, guilty of rape, banished to the Plantations for life, at Aberdeen 23.7.1764.
#875	Ritchie, Captain Crawford, from Aberdeen to Carolina 10.1764.

Jean Campbell, guilty of child murder, banished to the
Plantations for 14 years, at Ayr 10.1764.

#880　　　James Grant or Gordon, late a soldier in the Scots Lowlander
or Queen's Regiment, guilty of housebreaking and theft,
banished to the Plantations for 14 years, 11.1764.

#881　　　Patrick Gellie Farquhar, Captain of the 66th Regiment of Foot,
commanded by Lord Adam Gordon, died in Jamaica
1764.

#885　　　"For New York. Jean, a brigantine of two years old, an 140
ton burthen, Captain William Spark, will sail wind and
weather serving, from the Port of Aberdeen upon 20
January next, and will receive passengers on moderate
terms, for the transportation of whom the ship is well
accommodated. Such are inclined to embrace this
opportunity may apply to the said Captain William Spark
or to William Brebner and Company, merchants in
Aberdeen." 24.12.1764.

#892　　　"House carpenters, wheelwrights or masons who incline to go
abroad and settle in Grenada, on applying to Alexander
Lumsden, advocate in Aberdeen, will meet with proper
encouragement." 11.2.1765.

Jean, Captain Spark, from Aberdeen to New York 11.2.1765.

#893　　　Friendship, Captain Mackie, arrived in Aberdeen from Virginia
with tobacco, 18.2.1765.

#901　　　"That there is now wanted to go to the island of Grenada in
the West Indies, two or three able bodied young men
bred to the mason trade, to serve a mason now settled
on that island, who lately went from this place - any
person willing to go, by applying to William Smith, writer
in Aberdeen, will meet with good encouragement."
15.4.1765.

"Last week came into the Tay, a ship from Philadelphia with
lintseed. When she was about 300 leagues from that
port the master Thomas Greig and a boy were washed
overboard and drowned." 15.4.1765.

906　　　Public notice regarding the sale of lands by the Crown in
Grenada, the Grenades, Tobago, St Vincent and
Dominica. 5.1765.

Katherine Finlay, daughter of Robert Finlay a weaver in
Falkirk, guilty of child murder, was banished to the
Plantations for life, at Falkirk 5.1765.

# 908	Alexander McEan or Cameron, a cattle thief, was banished to the Plantations for life; Mary McFerson was banished to the Plantations for life. Both to be transmitted from sheriff to sheriff until they arrive in Glasgow in order from thence to be transported, at Inverness 5.1765. Christian Robinson, a pickpocket, banished to the Plantations for life, at Perth 5.1765.
#909	Jane, Captain Sparks, arrived in New York from Aberdeen 1765.
#914	Industry, Captain Deas, arrived in Aberdeen from Virginia, 15.7.1765.
#915	James Baillie, schoolmaster in Dundee, guilty of forging banknotes, to be pilloried then banished to the Plantations for life, 12.7.1765.
#924	John Davidson to be whipped through Aberdeen then banished to the Plantations for 7 years, at Aberdeen 23.9.1765. James McIntosh, servant to James Smith a dyer in Newmill, Keith, Banffshire, guilty of theft and housebreaking, was banished to the Plantations for life, at Aberdeen 10.1765. Robert Reid, guilty of robbery, was banished to the Plantations for 14 years, at Glasgow 9.1765.
#925	John Ban Cameron or McIllony, in Struan after in Lockerbie then in Argyll, guilty of cattle theft, was banished to the Plantations for life, at Perth 9.1765.
#927	"On Friday last John Davidson and James Macintosh were sent off under guard to Glasgow in order to be transported to America, the first for 7 years and the other for life" 14.10.1765.
#930	Edinburgh, 4.11.1765. "On Monday last the University of Edinburgh conferred the degree of Doctor of Physic on Mr Corbin Griffin from Virginia."
#933	Edinburgh, 20.11.1765. "On Saturday last the following gentlemen had the degree of Doctor of Physics conferred on them by the University of Edinburgh - Mr Thomas Rushton, Philadelphia, and Mr Archibald Campbell, South Carolina."
#938	General Murray, Captain Thain, arrived in Aberdeen from Virginia, 30.12.1765.
#942	"Wanted a house carpenter, a blacksmith, and a mason to serve in Antigua for 4 years. Any such who are good

tradesmen and well recommended may apply to George Moir of Scotstown at Aberdeen who will give them good encouragement." 27.1.1766.

#945   Edinburgh, 8.2.1766. This day James Baillie indicted for forging the British Linen Company notes, Capraisse Goose the French valet for wounding and maltreating a gentleman's servants, and Alexander Mitchell for theft, were carried from [Edinburgh] Tolbooth and taken to Glasgow for transportation to HM Plantations in America.

#948   "Wanted several house carpenters and blacksmiths who will enter into debentures to serve in the West Indies. Any such properly recommended may apply to John Durno, advocate in Aberdeen, who will give sutable encouragement." 10.3.1766.

#957   William Cunningham, son of William Cunningham a land labourer in Stewarton, guilty of burglary, was banished to the Plantations for 7 years, while William McCaull in Cotthouse of Glenluce, a thief, was banished to the Plantations for 7 years, at Ayr 7.5.1766.

#958   James Cockburn in Greenfaulds, a thief, was banished to America for 14 years, at Glasgow 1.5.1766.

#959   Alexander Keir, servant to George Birnie in Faskane, parish of Rathen, Banffshire, a thief, was banished to the Plantations for 14 years, at Aberdeen 5.1766.

George Wilson or Gordon, in Saugh of Deer, parish of New Deer, a housebreaker, was banished to the Plantations for life, at Aberdeen 5.1766.

"For Virginia, the good ship Harriot, Thomas Herdman commander, now lying at Aberdeen Harbour, extremely well fitted for passengers, will be ready to sail the 15th without fail. Mr Durward, or the master, to be spoke with every day in the Exchange." 26.5.1766.

#959   Alexander Rob, Walter Annesley and John Blair, thieves in Banff, were banished to the Plantations for life, Mary Lawson, child murderer, was also banished to the Plantations for life, at Aberdeen 5.1766.

#961   The Reverend William Nisbet, minister of Firth and Stenness in Orkney, guilty of adultery, was sentenced to be transported and banished to the Plantations for life, at Inverness 25.5.1766.

63

#964	"Last Tuesday Alexander Ross, George Wilson, Alexander Keir, Mary Lawson and William Riddell were shipped for America." 30.6.1766.
#965	Harriot sailed for Virginia.
#967	"Captain Ramage of Leith, homeward bound with wood from Boston in New England, who struck the Cape about 12 miles from Arbroath, is got off without damage and arrived at Leith." 27.7.1766.
#969	"Arrived a sloop from Virginia with tobacco and timber." 4.11.1766.
#974	Jean McKandy, servant to John Lumsden of Cushnie, guilty of child murder, was banished to the Plantations, at Aberdeen 9.1766.
#975	"For Antigua, the Grenades and Jamaica The Christie of Aberdeen a fine ship of 100 tons burthen ... taking goods and passengers .... on 15 November."
	"Wanted for the Granades. Two house carpenters or squarewrights and two gardeners. The house carpenters is wanted very good of their business and the gardeners if they are skilled in raising kitchen stuff will answer. For particulars enquire at George Wilson, merchant in Aberdeen."
#976	Grizel Buchanan, in Wellfield of Cathcart, a thief, was banished to the Plantations for 14 years, at Glasgow 17.9.1766.
#978	Christie of Aberdeen, a 100 ton sloop, from Aberdeen to Antigua, Grenada and Jamaica with "excellent accommodation for passengers", 15.11.1766
#979	"A young man that is qualified in wright work particularly making cabinets, tables, chairs etc, that will engage for 4 years to go to Jamaica will meet with good encouragement and usage upon applying to the publisher of this paper and have his passage paid to that place." 10.1766.
	"Any blacksmith, mason, wright or coppersmith who will engage to go to Jamaica and serve for 4 years will get good encouragement and may apply to Mr Duthie."
#981	Margaret MacWhirter, servant maid in Ballantrae, guilty of child murder, was banished to the Plantations for life, at Ayr 10.10.1766.

Matthew Stewart, an apprentice wright in Ayr, a thief, was banished to the Plantations for 14 years, at Ayr 10.10.1766.

#986   "Wanted two wrights and a mason to serve 4 years in the island of Antigua or Grenada. Any such who are masters of their business and well recommended may apply to George Moir of Scotstoun at Aberdeen." 12.1766.

#987   Marion Davy, guilty of child murder, was banished to the Plantations for life, at Edinburgh 30.11.1766.

Dr Alexander Moir, born in Mortlich, Banffshire, died in St Croix 11.1766.

#990   Duncan Kennedy, a thief, banished to the Plantations for 7 years, at Haddington 12.1767.

"That the ship Christie, Robert Gill master, for the Grenades and Jamaica sails precisely the 30th January next, all those who have any goods to send by the vessel will have them shipped before that time and the passengers will have a note of their names with Captain Gill on or before the 3rd day of January next and acquaint him if they intend a cabin or steerage passage that necessaries may be provided accordingly."   12.1767

#991   "For Kingston in Jamaica the Britannia, Archibald McLarty master, now lying in Greenock, will be ready to take goods on board by 15th of January and clear to sail by 15th February. For freight or passage please apply to Fisher and Ballantine, Glasgow. The Britannia has very good accommodation for passengers. She will call at Cork or any of the Leeward Islands if a freight offers." 1.1767

#995   "On Saturday last, Jean McKandy banished at the last Circuit court for child murder, was shipped at this place for the Granades." 2.2.1767

#1000   "On 24 December last died in Antigua Dr Grainger an eminent physician." 3.1767

#1001   John MacRae, James Hamilton and William Rannie, thieves, were banished to the Plantations for 7 years, while Marion Brown from Kirkcudbright, a child murderer, was banished for 14 years, at Edinburgh 3.1767

#1003   Harriet, Herdman, sailed from Aberdeen to Virginia 3.1767

#1005   Mr Daniel McLean, late merchant in Glasgow, was appointed as Customs Collector at Montego Bay, Jamaica, 4.1767.

#1009   "On 31 December last, died the Reverend Dr James Moir of Edgecombe County, North Carolina, who has left his estate to his brother Reverend Mr Henry Moir of Auchtertool."

Angus Cameron, aged around 20, servant to an innkeeper in Strontian, a thief, was banished to the Plantations for life, at Inveraray 5.1767.

#1010   George Young, a housebreaker from Stonehaven, was banished to the Plantations for life, at Perth 5.1767.

Reverend Messrs Nathaniel Whitaker and Samson Occum, ministers of the Gospel in New England, arrived in Edinburgh to raise funds for Reverend Mr Whitelock's school for Indians.

#1011   Margaret Douglas, servant to John Scoon in Netherthornywhat, was banished to the Plantations for life, at Dumfries 20.5.1767

Alexander Taylor was ordered to be transported for life, William Roy, a wheelwright in Huntly, and James Cook, a dyer in Huntly, rioters, were sentenced to transportation for life, William Grant and William Barclay, rioters in West Folds of Glass, were sentenced to be transported for life, at Aberdeen 5.1767

#1013   Duncan McDonald, in Connachan of Glen Moriston, a thief, was banished to the Plantations for 14 years; John Bain or Miller in Shurririve, Caithness, a thief, was banished to the Plantations; George Whier, a tailor in Sarclet, Caithness, a thief, was banished to the Plantation for life, at Inverness 23.5.1767

#1015   "Wanted for Jamaica. Two masons and two wrights thoroughly qualified in their business and of exceptional good character. Such being well recommended will meet with good encouragement by applying to Alexander Milne jr, merchant in Aberdeen." 22.6.1767

"Monday last William Grant, William Barclay and John Morison were sent under guard for Glasgow in order to be transported to America in terms of their sentence.." 22.6.1767

#1017   "We hear that the University of St Andrews has conferred the degree of Doctor of Divinity on the Reverend Mr Nathaniel Whitaker from America."
"Wanted for Pensacola in West Florida. Four house carpenters and two bricklayers who will find good encouragement on applying to Alexander Ross jr., merchant in Aberdeen." 7.1767

#1018   "The University of Edinburgh has been pleased to confer the degree of Doctor of Divinity on the Reverend Mr Eleazor Wheelock, founder and president of the academy for the education of Indian youth in New England." 25.7.1767

#1020   "Sir Archibald Grant bart. of Monymusk has got a grant of several thousand acres of land in the Floridas and is sending over a surveyor and servants ..." 7.1767

#1024   "Wanted for Jamaica a blacksmith, a coppersmith, a miller, two wrights or house carpenters. Such being good tradesmen and well recommended will have good encouragement on applying to Alexander Milne jr., merchant in Aberdeen." 8.1767

#1027   Christie, Gill, arrived in Aberdeen from Jamaica, 9.1767

#1029   Alexander Campbell, Captain of the 62nd Foot and a Major in Portuguese Service, died in Tobago 7.1767

#1030   James Hogg, a butcher in Falkirk, guilty of cow-stealing, was banished to the Plantations for 7 years, at Stirling 9.1767

#1031   Agnes Dugald, Anderston, Glasgow, guilty of child murder, was banished to the Plantations for life; John Steel, an apprentice tailor in Lanark, guilty of attempted murder, was banished to the Plantations for life, at Glasgow 9.1767

#1033   Jean, Brown, arrived at Aberdeen from Jamaica, and the Harriot, Herdman, arrived in Aberdeen from Virginia, 9.1767

#1035   Christie, Gill, from Aberdeen to Jamaica 10.1767

#1041   "For Madeira, Barbados, Grenada, Antigua and Virginia - the good ship Harriot, Thomas Herdman commander, burthen 200 tons, now lying in the harbour of Aberdeen, will be ready to sail against the 20th February next. She has excellent accommodation for passengers who may depend on being well used. For particulars apply the master." 12.1767

67

#1044 James Burrow, late of the Customs in Glasgow, appointed as a Revenue Officer in America, 7.1.1768

Harriot, 200 tons, master Thomas Herdman, from Aberdeen to Madeira, Barbados, Antigua and Virginia 20.2.1768, "she has excellent accommodation for passengers, who may depend on being well used"

#1045 Alexander Anderson, late in Burnt Brae, Old Deer, sentenced to banishment for life in 1754, was whipped through Aberdeen and then imprisoned until an opportunity arose to transport him, 1.1768

#1048 "Wanted for Grenada, a mason, a millwright and a housekeeper. Any such, well recommended, will find good encouragement, by applying to Alexander Ross jr., merchant in Aberdeen." 8.2.1768.

#1050 On Wednesday last died here {Edinburgh} Mr William McDonald, late of Jamaica, 2.1768

#1051 Alexander Anderson, a forger banished to the Plantations, was sent from Aberdeen to Edinburgh, 2.1768

#1054 Edinburgh, on Wednesday last James Main and George Garnock were sentenced to be whipped and banished to America for life, 21.3.1768

#1055 Wanted for Jamaica, two wrights, well qualified in their business, who on applying any time this week to William Nicoll, advocate in Aberdeen, will have suitable wages and encouragement, 28.3.1768.

#1059 "For the James River, Virginia, the ship George, master Peter Paterson, now lying in the harbour of Aberdeen will be clear to sail by the 25 May next. For freight and passage, apply to the master." 25.4.1768.

Glasgow. Two Indian chiefs belonging to the province of Connecticut, lately arrived here in a vessel from New York, 25.4.1768

Alexander Gordon in Kirktown of Cabrach, found guilty of theft, was sentenced to be whipped and banished to the Plantations for life, Aberdeen 4.1768.

Evan McGregor in Kirkmichael, Banff, his wife Janet MacPherson, and Isabel McGregor his sister, found guilty of sheepstealing. Isabel McGregor successfully petitioned to be banished to the Plantations for 14 years, Aberdeen 4.1768.

Extract of a letter from Pensacola to a gentleman in Aberdeen 26.2.1768.

#1063   "Edinburgh. We are advised that from the western islands of
Scotland, that a number of settlers have lately
embarked for America from these islands, in particular
betwixt 40 and 50 families have gone from the island of
Jura alone for Cape Fear in Carolina to settle
thereabouts and in Georgia. Some of them are persons
in good circumstances." 22.5.1768.

Margaret Boyne from Elgin, found guilty of child murder, was
banished to the Plantations for life, Inverness 5.1768.

John Grant alias Brachader, in Rictian, found guilty of
horsetheft, and Charles Stewart in Cromdale, found
guilty of cattle theft, were banished to the Plantations for
14 years, Inverness 5.1768.

#1065   George, Paterson, from Aberdeen to Virginia 6.1768.

#1069   "Wanted to go to a wholesome and good settlement in the
West Indies, one housewright, one millwright and 2
masons who by timeously applying to Francis Leys,
merchant in Aberdeen, will hear of very good
encouragement." 4.7.1768.

"We are informed that about 35 different families are
immediately to sail from Argyllshire to North Carolina in
order to settle there." 4.7.1768.

#1072   Aberdeen, on Saturday last Alexander Gordon and Isobel
McGregor banished to the Plantations, were sent to
Glasgow to be shipped for that purpose. 25.7.1768.

Extract from a letter from Montserrat to a gentleman in
Glasgow, 8.6.1768, discussing a negro insurrection on
the island.

#1080   Donald Rugg, late tenant in Freswick, found guilty of
housebreaking and theft, a prisoner in Inverness
Tolbooth, was sentenced to be whipped through Wick
and then banished to the Plantations for life. Similarly
John Swanston, a Chelsea pensioner, found guilty of
the same charges, was to be whipped through Thurso
and then banished to the Plantations for life, 9.1768.

#1081   Advice is received from Virginia of the safe arrival of the
Harriot, Captain Herdman. 26.9.1768.

#1086   "Wanted immediately to go abroad to the island of St Vincent
in the West Indies the following tradesmen, viz. 4
masons, 4 housewrights, and 2 millwrights, sober
young men that have a thorough knowledge of their
business ... apply to James Watson, advocate in

Aberdeen, Mr McGhie, New Inn, Aberdeen, or Mr Alexander Bruce, merchant in Banff." 31.10.1768.

#1086 "Aberdeen. Yesterday were brought to town and committed to prison, Donald Rugg, late tenant in Freswick, John Swanston, Chelsea pensioner in Thurso, George Wheir, tailor in Sarfet, Margaret Boyne, resident in Elgin, who were this day sent to Glasgow under armed guard in terms of their banishment." 31.10.1768.

#1088 "Mr John Scott of Virginia was lately married to Miss Betty Gordon, daughter of Mr Thomas Gordon, professor of Philosophy at King's College, Aberdeen." 14.11.1768.

#1089 "Harriot of Aberdeen, Captain Herdman, from Virginia with a cargo of tobacco was wrecked on the Island of Sanday, Orkney, 21.10.1768, all the crew was drowned." 21.11.1768.

"George, Paterson, arrived in Glasgow from Virginia in 31 days." 21.11.1768.

#1092 Extract from a letter from a gentleman in Pensacola to a gentleman in Aberdeen 20.8.1768

#1096 "For Kingston in Jamaica, to call at Madeira, Grenada, and Antigua. The Janet and Ann, master George Craik, a new vessel burthen about 140 tons; has good accommodation for passengers and sails from Aberdeen the 20th of February next. For freight of passage apply to Alexander Young or George Wilson, merchants in Aberdeen. N.B. the vessel takes in wine as freight in Madeira for Aberdeen - wrights and masons, properly qualifed and well recommended, that are willing to serve in Grenada will meet with good encouragement upon applying as above." 9.1.1769.

#1102 "Wanted. An experienced house carpenter of good character, for a gentleman in Jamaica, very good encouragement will be given upon applying to Alexander Milne, merchant in Aberdeen. But none need apply unless unexceptionally well qualified and well recommended." 20.2.1769

#1103 "House carpenters, well recommended, and willing to engage to serve for a few years in the island of Dominica, will hear of good encouragement on applying immediately to John Burnett, merchant in Aberdeen." 27.2.1769

#1105 "Wanted a house carpenter to go to Antigua, such a one, if well recommended for sobriety, honesty and capacity will get great encouragement, by applying to John Still, merchant in Aberdeen. N.B. The person applying would be more acceptable if he understood somewhat of the cartwright business." 13.3.1769

#1109   Janet and Anne, Craik, sailed from Aberdeen to Jamaica 10.4.1769.

#1115   William Robertson, a merchant or shopkeeper in Aberdeen, found guilty of theft, was banished to the Plantations for 7 years, at Aberdeen 22.5.1769. Hugh McLeod, alias James McBain, a thief and a housebreaker, and James Gordon in Ordrettan, a horsethief, were banished to the Plantations for life, in Aberdeen 17.5.1769

#1117   William Chatto, a saddler in Kelso, a prisoner in Jedburgh Tolbooth, found guilty of attempted murder, was banished to the Plantations for life, at Jedburgh 16.5.1769.

#1123   "Wanted for St Augustine in East Florida. Two house carpenters and one mason to indent for 4 years. Any such well recommended will find good encouragement by applying to Alexander Ross jr., merchant in Aberdeen." 17.7.1769.

#1124   Extract from a letter from a gentleman in Philadelphia to his friend in Edinburgh 24.5.1769.

#1127   Extract of a letter from Pensacola to a gentleman in Aberdeen
#1128   Charming Janet, master ... Brown, arrived in Aberdeen from Virginia, 21.8.1769.

#1255   Janet Abernethy, a thief, was banished to America for life, Aberdeen 27.1.1772.

#1133   Alexander Grant of Arndilly was married in Edinburgh to Helenora, daughter of William Murray late of Jamaica, 18.9.1769.

James Sands, a merchant in Charleston, died there 3.8.1769.

#1141   An extract from a letter from Williamsburg, Virginia, 14.9.1769 "Masons, housekeepers and 1 millwright, properly qualified and willing to serve 4 years in Grenada or Tobago, will meet with good encouragement on applying to George Wilson, merchant in Aberdeen. N.B. George Wilson has just now imported fine flavor Jamaica and Grenada rum which he sells retail and wholesale at reasonable prices." 20.11.1769.

#1143   "Masons and blacksmiths, house carpenters and millwrights, properly qualified and willing to serve 4 years in

Grenada or Dominica, will meet with good encouragement by applying to John Durno, advocate in Aberdeen." 4.12.1769

"For Tobago, Grenada and Jamaica the ship Janet and Anne, George Craik master, it has excellent accommodation for passengers and sails from Aberdeen 20.2.1770. For freight and passage apply to George Wilson or Garioch and Young, merchants in Aberdeen." 4.12.1769.

#1144 "There was one James Gray who it is supposed left Aberdeen years ago and went to Jamaica and stayed there some time, then went to the Grenades where he soon died. If his parents or near relatives are still alive and will apply to Ninian Johnston, merchant in Aberdeen, where they will hear of something to their advantage." 11.12.1769.

"If the nearest relations of one David Allen who went abroad from Aberdeenshire about 15 or 20 years ago and died in Antigua in 1760, apply to John Durno, advocate in Aberdeen, where they will learn something to their advantage." 11.12.1769.

#1148 Mrs Jean Mercer, spouse to Mr David Alves in Quebec, died in Edinburgh 7.1.1770.

#1150 "Masons and blacksmiths, housecarpenters and millwrights, properly qualified and willing to serve four years in Grenada or Dominica, will meet with good encouragement by applying to John Durno, advocate in Aberdeen." 22.1.1770

#1151 The ship Lady Margaret, bound for the James River, Virginia, stranded at Pencorse near Hunterston, 25.1.1770.

#1156 "For Grenada. The ship Janet and Ann, George Craik master, sails from Aberdeen 20th current. For freight and passage apply to George Wilson and Garioch & Young, merchants in Aberdeen, or to Captain Craik." 4.1770.

#1165 Peter Kilgour in Ardoch, Banchory, a horse thief, was banished to the Plantations for life, at Aberdeen 21.5.1770.

#1170 Andrew Wilson, founder in Aberfoyle, and his wife Janet Graeme or Ogilvy, found guilty of theft, were banished to the Plantations for life, Perth 30.5.1770.

#1176   Janet and Ann, Craik, has arrived in the Grenades after a passage of 6 weeks and 2 days, all well on board, 23.7.1770.

#1180   Extract of a letter from a gentleman in St Augustine to his friend in Aberdeen, dated 23.5.1770, regarding military activity there.

#1181   "Edinburgh, 25.8.1770. We are informed, that since the month of April last, six large ships have sailed from the Western Islands and other parts of the Highlands, all of them full of passengers for North Carolina in order to settle in that colony; at a moderate computation, it is thought, that of men, women and children, no fewer than 1200 have embarked on the above ships."

Extract of a letter from New York to a merchant in Glasgow re trade.

#1183   Mary McDonald alias Henderson alias McEan , tailor, guilty of child murder, was banished to the Plantations for life, at Inverness 1.9.1770.

Margaret Anderson, wife of John Copland tenant in Upper Mains of Allardyce in the parish of Arbuthnott, guilty of theft, was banished to the Plantations in America for 7 years, at Aberdeen 6.9.1770.

#1184   Walter Anderson, a weaver in Portsoy, in the parish of Fordyce, Banffshire, guilty of theft, was banished to the Plantations in America for 14 years, at Aberdeen 10.9.1770.

#1185   "Wanted for Antigua. Cart and Mill wrights, such are capable of these branches and willing to go abroad may hear of good encouragement, by applying to Mr Thibou in the Green, or Mr Alexander Smith, merchant in Aberdeen, N.B. they must be well recommended." 24.9.1770.

#1186   Aberdeen Infirmary Collections included a donation from Dr Robert Harvey from Antigua of 10 guineas, 1.10.1770.

#1192   Janet and Ann, master George Craik, arrived in Aberdeen from the Grenades via Leith, 2.11.1770.

#1193   Ritchie, master Malcolm Crawford, bound from Virginia to Greenock with a cargo of tobacco was forced into Campbelltown by gales, where all of the crew except the master, the 2 mates and a boy were taken by the Press Gang, 11.11.1770.

#1194	Mally of Montrose, Captain Hume, returned to Montrose from Newfoundland after a successful 6 month fishing voyage, 26.11.1770.
#1195	Aurora, Lyon, arrived in the Clyde from Virginia, 5.12.1770.
#1196	"For Madeira, Tobago, Grenada, and Jamaica. The ship Janet and Ann, George Craik master, now lying to at Aberdeen, for goods and passengers, sails the first day of February next. For freight or passage apply to George Wilson or to Garioch and Young, merchants in Aberdeen, or to Captain Craik." 10.12.1770.
	Caesar of Glasgow, Captain Slingsby, from Newcastle to America with convicts was lost on the coast of Kent 29.11.1770 - the crew and passengers saved.
#1197	John Harvey of Aberdeen, who had acquired a fortune in the West Indies, died in London 8.12.1770.
#1203	Britannia, Lawrie, from Honduras to the Clyde, was wrecked off Cuba 10.1770.
#1207	Dr Francis Garden, died in Charleston, South Carolina, 10.1770.
	Extract of a letter from a gentleman in St Croix to a friend in Glasgow, dated St Kitts 17.12.1770, stating that Kennedy and Marshall, the factors in Porto Rico, were imprisoned by the Spanish and then taken to St Croix.
#1208	Edinburgh, 25.2.1771. "We are informed from the Western Islands that upwards of 500 souls from Islay and the adjacent islands are preparing to emigrate next summer to America, under the conduct of a gentleman of wealth and merit, whose predecessors resided in Islay for many centuries past. And that there is a large colony of the most wealthy and substantive people in Skye making ready to follow the example of the Argathelians in going to the fertile and cheap lands on the other side of the Atlantic Ocean. It is to be dreaded that these migrations will prove hurtful to the mother country and therefore its friends ought to use every proper method to prevent them."
	Extract of a letter from a gentleman in Philadelphia to his friend in Edinburgh refering to Mr Kirkland, a missionary supported by the Society in Scotland for the Propagation of Christian Knowledge, and his work among the Oneida Indians. Edinburgh 27.2.1771.

#1210   "Culture of Flax. Wanted to go to Boston in New England a young man well qualified in raising of flax and bring it to proper maturity. They may apply to the printer of this journal, where they will meet with proper encouragement." 18.3.1771

#1217   Janet Dunlop, sometime servant to John Wintrop, tenant in Craggs, parish of Lilliesleaf, Roxburghshire, found guilty of child murder and banished to America for life, Jedburgh 5.1771.

Mary Wilson in Paisley, and Margaret Granger, daughter of Robert Granger a weaver in Paisley, guilty of theft, banished to the Plantations for 14 years, Glasgow 5.1771.

James Miln in Kirriemuir, guilty of murder, banished to America for 7 years, Perth 5.1771.

Alexander Hill in Boyndie, guilty of theft, banished to the Plantations for 14 years, Aberdeen 5.1771.

#1220   Aberdeen. "Tuesday last landed here from on board the Portland, Wilson, (7 weeks and 4 days from Charleston, South Carolina) the Hon. Egerton Leigh and family." 27.5.1771.

#1227   Extract from a letter from a gentleman in Norfolk, Virginia, to his friend in Glasgow 30.5.1771, re events in North Carolina, the Regulators, and the actions of Governor Tryon.

#1227   Extract from a letter from a gentleman at Osburne's Warehouse, Virginia, to his friend in Glasgow, 27.5.1771, re flood damage.

#1232   Captain James Hamilton of the 10th Regiment, died in Quebec 7.4.1771.

#1233   John McKitterick, carter at Bridgend, Dumfries, guilty of rioting, banished to the Plantations for 7 years; Andrew Wilson, tailor in Dumfries, guilty of rioting, banished to the Plantations for 7 years; William Milligan, weaver in Dumfries, guilty of rioting, banished to the Plantations for 3 years, at Edinburgh 12.8.1771.

#1236   Extracts of letters from Charleston which had arrived at Leith on the ship Minerva 10.9.1771, re the trial of the regulators at Wilmington and to the Virginia floods.

Extract of a letter from a gentleman in Antigua to a friend in Glasgow, 25.7.1771, re the slave insurrection in Tobago.

#1237	Edinburgh. "We hear from the island of Skye that no less than 370 persons have lately embarked from that island in order to settle in North Carolina; several of them are people of property who intend making purchases of land in America. The late great rise of the rents in the western islands of Scotland is said to be the reason for this emigration." 9.1771.
#1237	Bell or Belinda, born in Bengal, a servant of John Johnston of Hangingshaws, resident in Balgonie, Fife, guilty of child murder, banished to the Plantations in America or the West Indies for life, at Perth 9.1771.
	Jenny, Captain Fullerton, arrived in the Clyde from Virginia, 4.1771.
#1238	William Brown to be whipped and banished to the Plantations for life; George Philip, abortionist, banished to the Plantations for life; Janet Abernethy, daughter of William Abernethy in Old Manse of Foveran, guilty of theft, banished to the Plantations for life, at Aberdeen 9.1771.
#1242	Extract of a letter from St Croix 15.7.1771 to a friend in Aberdeen re a trial in St Croix.
#1245	"Wanted. A housewright to go to one of the Leeward Islands in the West Indies. For further particulars apply to Mr James Skeen in Upper Kirkgate." 11.11.1771.
#1245	John and Jean, Captain Baxter, arrived in Aberdeen from Virginia with tobacco 10.11.1771.
	Extract from a letter from a gentleman in Jamaica to a friend in Edinburgh re a Jamaican ship, Captain Scott, which was seized by the Spanish who murdered the captain and crew, Edinburgh 15.11.1771.
#1248	Janet and Anne, Captain Craik, arrived in Aberdeen from Jamaica with rum, 3.12.1771.
#1249	"Wanted. A surgeon and 2 or 3 coopers who will engage to serve in their respective employments for 4 years, upon an estate in Antigua. Any such whose character and qualifications are well recommended may apply to George Moir of Scotston, Aberdeen, who will give them suitable encouragement." 16.12.1771.
#1256	"Wanted, a surgeon, two or three coopers, a mason, a house carpenter and a young man who has been used to the farming business, all to serve in the way of their respective employment for 4 years in Antigua. Any such whose characters and qualifications are well

	recommended, may apply to George Moir of Scotstown in Aberdeen who will give them suitable encouragement." 3.2.1772.
#1258	"Wants employment in New England or the neighboring colonies. A millwright, well recommended, and fully capable of the branch he professes. Enquire at the publisher." 17.2.1772.
#1260	Thomas Sheridan, a soldier, and Edward Armstrong, a drummer, both of the 17th Regiment of Foot, guilty of theft, were banished to the Plantations for life, Edinburgh 26.2.1772.
#1261	"Wanted. One or two cooper lads, to engage for 3 or 4 years, to their business in Canada. For particulars apply to Gilbert Glenny, merchant in Aberdeen, where they will find his brother who engages them. This advertisement is not to be repeated as his brother returns home to Quebeck 10 or 12 days after this." 9.3.1772.
#1262	Glasgow, 11.3.1772. John Donaldson was banished to the Plantations for life on 9.3.1772.
#1263	Glasgow, 16.3.1772. "On Thursday last a number of convicts was brought to town from Edinburgh, in order to be shipped off for America, in terms of their sentences."
#1271	Jean Paterson, servant to John Youngson stabler in Aberdeen, guilty of deforcing and beating some Revenue Officers last July, banished to the Plantations, at Aberdeen 5.1772.
	Jane Baillie alias McDonald or Graham alias Jane Wilson alias Stewart, resident in Berwick Spital, guilty of pickpocketing at Duns Fair, was banished to the Plantations for life, at Jedburgh 5.1772.
#1272	William Mann, weaver in Aberdeen, John Gibbon, Chelsea pensioner in Aberdeen, Benjamin Lindsay, weaver in Aberdeen, John Clark, weaver in Aberdeen, William Hosie or Hosack, weaver in Aberdeen, all guilty of conspiracy to murder, were banished to the Plantations, the first two for life and the others for 10 years. Jean Paterson, above, was banished to the Plantations for 7 years. James Smith, weaver in Kinninmonth, guilty of theft and housebreaking, was banished to the Plantations for life. At Aberdeen 25.7.1772.

"The emigration from the Highlands of Scotland begin now to wear a serious aspect as they threaten to leave these extensive   tracks of our country desolate without a soul to cultivate or improve them..... I myself have this day been witness to an emigration from Sutherland - 19 or 20 families marched by land through Moray to Findhorn, from there they take ship for Leith, from Leith to Glasgow and there embark for America .... They are about 60 in number of different ages and sexes.." 20.5.1772.

#1277   "On Tuesday was brought here from Inverness Ann McDonald, under sentence of banishment by the Judiciary Court, and   next day together with John Gibbons, William Mann, William Hosie, John Clark, Benjamin Lindsay, James Smith and Jean Paterson were sent off to Glasgow to be thence transported in terms of their respective sentences." 29.6.1772.

"We hear from Dundee that last week arrived there, upwards of 100 emigrants with about 30 children, mostly on the breast, from the County of Sutherland, on their way to Greenock to procure passage to America. They say that many more will follow their example. They alledge the same reason for the conduct of the former emigrants from Skye, to wit, the enormous price of all sorts of provisions and the oppression of their superiors." 29.6.1772.

#1280   Edinburgh, 17.7.1772, "we hear from Greenock that a large ship has been freighted at that place, to carry 300 passengers from the Isle of Skye to Carolina."

"On Monday last passed through Kincardine O'Neil about 90 men, women and children, all from the shire of Sutherland on their way to Glasgow from where they are to embark for America. Not above 3 in the whole company could speak English and even these imperfectly." 7.1772.

#1281   "The emigrations from Sutherland and the environs still continues; several detachments of these voluntary exiles past the Spey on Thursday and Friday last on their way to Greenock." 27.7.1772.

#1282   "For Barbados, Tobago, Grenada, St Vincent, St Kitts and Antigua. The brig Christie, George Craik master, sails the 24th current, for freight and passage apply to the master on the Exchange, on board the ship or at Mr John Walker's, merchant at the corner of Marischal

Street, Aberdeen. N.B. as the master is well acquainted in the above islands any persons capable of keeping accompts or being well recommended as house carpenters or masons will find good encouragement by applying as above." 3.8.1772.

#1286 "James Elder Esq., of Dominica, who lately came over to London for the recovery of his health, died there on the 17th current." 31.8.1772.

"For Grenada and Jamaica. The ship Janet and Anne, John Yule master, has good accommodation for passengers and will sail from Aberdeen in December. For freight or passage apply to George Walker or Garioch and Young, merchants in Aberdeen." 31.8.1772

#1287 Edinburgh, 4.9.1772. an extract of a letter from a gentleman in the Western Isles dated 16 August. "The people who have emigrated from this poor corner of Scotland since the year 1768 have carried with them at least £10,000 in specie notwithstanding this is a great loss to us yet the depopulation by these emigrations is much greater. Unless some speedy remedy is fallen upon by the government and land holders the consequences must prove to be very fatal, as this part of the country is rather in the infancy of being civilised then improved, besides the continual emigrations from Ireland and Scotland will soon render our colonies independent on the mother country."

#1287 "Wanted for Grenada. A house carpenter well recommended; he will get good encouragement and may apply to James Duff, Sheriff Clerk of Banff, or to Alexander Duthie, advocate in Aberdeen." 7.9.1772.

"For Tobago, Grenada and Kingston in Jamaica, the brig Christie, George Craik master, will certainly sail from Aberdeen 25th current. Housecarpenters, millwrights and masons that choose to come under indenture will meet with good encouragement by applying to the Master. All gentlemen intending to go as passengers are requested to be in Aberdeen by the 20th current." 7.9.1772.

#1290 Chester, Captain Thomson, arrived at Aberdeen from Maryland with tobacco 26.9.1772.

"For Annapolis or Chestertown in Maryland near Philadelphia. The brigantine Chester, John Thomson master, will sail the 20th October. The vessel is a prime sailor and has excellent accommodation for passengers. For freight or passage apply to the master on Change at Change hours or at the house of Alexander Masson vintner. A few mechanicks such as taylors, bricklayers, plasterers, wrights, watchmakers, farriers, blacksmiths or any others who choose to go will meet with great encouragement, on applying to the above." 28.9.1772.

#1291   Donald Bain or McLeod and William McWilliam, servants in Borrowton, Caithness, guilty of housebreaking and theft, were banished to the Plantations for life. William Elder, tenant in Ifauld, his son Donald, and Alexander McDonald, guilty of fireraising, were to be publicly whipped and then banished to the Plantations for life, at Inverness 9.1772.

#1292   Lachlan Will or McLean was sentenced to be publicly whipped and then banished to the Plantations for life, at Aberdeen 10.1772.

#1293   "To be sold. One fourth concern in a Sugar Estate in the island of Tobago being the property of the heirs of one of the partners lately deceased. Above 60 acres are cultivated and partly planted in canes; there is a stock of Negroes on the estate, and the improvements and cultivation going on successfully. Any young gentleman inclined to reside on the estate for a few years will be preferred and a suitable salary allowed him. For further particulars enquire at Messrs Walker and Strachan, merchants in Edinburgh, or at James Kettle, writer there." 10.1772.

John Melvil, a tinker, and Mary Wilson wife of Charles Stewart a tinker, guilty of stealing shirts, were banished to the Plantations for 7 years, at Perth 10.1772. Peter Lawson, a weaver in Torryburn, and Colin Henderson, a smith there, guilty of housebreaking, were banished to the Plantations, at Perth 10.1772. Daniel Sutherland, a vagrant, guilty of pickpocketing, sentenced to be publicly whipped in Perth and then banished to the Plantations for life, at Perth 10.1772. Mary Spence, servant to ... Spence a tailor in Edinburgh, guilty of stealing clothes, was banished to the Plantations for life, at Perth 10.1772.

William Gray, a soldier of the 31st Regiment, guilty of theft and housebreaking, was banished to the Plantations for life, at Jedburgh 10.1772.

#1295 John Thomson alias Charles Grant, a thief and housebreaker, was banished to the Plantations for life, Ayr 27.10.1772.

#1297 "Wanted for Antigua. Several millwrights. Any such properly recommended will meet with good encouragement in applying to Alexander Smith, merchant in the Green, Aberdeen." 11.1772.

Chester, Captain Thomson, sailed from Aberdeen to Chestertown, Maryland, 8.11.1772.

#1298 Edinburgh, 18.11.1772. "We hear from Wick that the two criminals Elder and McDonald lately convicted before the Circuit Court of Justiciary at Inverness for setting fire to the house of Mr James Hogg in Borlum were publicly whipped through the streets of Thurso on Friday 30th ultimate and at the market place of Wick on Friday following. Next day they set off under armed guard to be transported."

#1299 Aberdeen 30.11.1772. "On Tuesday last Donald Bain alias McLeod, William McWilliam, William and Donald Elder, Alexander McDonald, and Alexander Morison, all from Inverness Prison were sent off under guard for Stonehaven. The first mentioned five under banishment to America, the last A. Morison is to be carried to Edinburgh to be tried for theft. At the same time was transmitted from this prison Lauchlan Will alias McLean, sentenced at the last Circuit Court at this place to be banished to America for theft."

#1300 "Wanted 2 journeyman house carpenters, well qualified and properly recommended to go to St Vincent and bound to serve there for 3 to 4 years, will meet with good encouragement and if they behave well, have a good chance to succeed their master in his business. Apply to John Clark, advocate in Aberdeen." 7.12.1772.

#1301 "Wanted to oversee a plantation in the West Indies a young man, from 20 to 30 years of age who can be well recommended, and understands something of arithmetic and book-keeping. For particulars apply to Provost Jopp." 14.12.1772.

#1307 Janet and Ann, master John Yule, passage offered from Aberdeen to Grenada and Jamaica 13.3.1773

#1308	Sally, master James Patrick, passage offered from Dundee to Grenada 26.2.1773
#1333	"In the island of St John's in the Gulph of the St Lawrence, latitude 46`30' the choice estate of George Spence in St Peter's parish to be disposed of in the following manner. The tenants paying their own freight over and finding everything for themselves, viz. The first year after arrival one penny per acre, after three years at 6 pence per acre, after five years at one shilling per acre, after ten years at two shillings per acre and so to continue forever to them, their heirs or assignees - each family to have 100 acres. NB Mr Spence, as being the first adventurer, had his choice of land which is excellent with a deal of meadowland and good fishing of all sorts at the door; his son who has been on the island with his family these four years and carries on a great farm has now a fine water mill will be of great service to the tenants in assisting them. And Captain George Thomson can witness all this, having been there often and knows the truth of all. Enquire for Captain George Thomson at his house in Old Aberdeen" 26.7.1773.
#1341	The brigantine Christie, master George Craik, from Aberdeen to Tobago, Grenada and Jamaica with passengers 1.10.1773.
	"young gentlemen qualified for bookkeepers, house carpenters, millwrights and masons well recommended will meet with good encouragement"
	Extract from a letter from Maryburgh dated 4.9.1773 "upon the first of this month sailed from this port for America 425 men, women and children, all from Croydar, Lochaber, Appin and Mammore, Fort William included and Maryburgh ... they carried £6000 sterling in ready cash ... the country is thus deprived of its men and its wealth ... sole cause - extraordinary rents"
#1354	At Stornaway the David and Anne of Leith, master ... Ritchie, with emigrants from Morayshire bound for America, 9.1773.
#1355	"Wanted to go to Carolina. Two house carpenters and two blacksmiths to engage for 4 or 5 years. For particulars apply to John Durno, advocate in Aberdeen." 27.12.1773

#1356	Christie, master ... Craik, from Aberdeen to Jamaica 28.12.1773
	Letter from a settler in Nova Scotia
#1357	"The causes of emigration ..."
#1359	Letter from Argyll re emigration
#1360	"Wanted - several strong, healthy unmarried men and women from the ages of 16 to 30 to indent for 4 years to go to New York and Philadelphia. Those who incline to engage may apply to John Ross, writer in Aberdeen, who will inform them as to the encouragement and other particulars, 31.1.1774."
	Adventure, master Thomas Symmer, offered passage from Aberdeen to Barbados, Tobago, Grenada, etc, to sail 30.3.1774 {actually sailed 12.4.1774}
#1361	George of Leith, master ... Alexander, arrived in Charleston 20.11.1773
#1362	Letter from Williamsburg, Virginia, dated 25.11.1773, re Daniel McLeod of Kilmorie, a Scots gentleman, who had left for Albany on way to Beckman township near Lake Champlain, to view land he had bought on which he intended to settle families from Scotland.
#1363	"Wanted. A house carpenter who must also have some knowledge of mill work and will indent to go to the River Mississippi in West Florida. Any such well recommended will find suitable encouragement by applying to Alexander Ross, merchant in Aberdeen, 21.2.1774."
#1364	The ship Buchanan of Greenock, Captain James Moody, from New York to Bordeaux was lost near Bordeaux 22.1 1774.
#1365	"We are informed that Mr Wright, collector of North American plants and HM gardener at Quebec, will set out soon for Terra de Labradora, in order to make discoveries in that uncultivated and barren part of the world where no botanist ever was."
	"For St John's and Quebec. The ship John and Jane, burthen 250 tons, has excellent accommodation for passengers and will sail precisely towrds the end of this month. Any that incline may apply to Andrew Baxter the master, or William Durward, merchant in Aberdeen."

#1368	A letter from New York concerning the condition of the passengers from Sutherland on board the brig Nancy, 1.1774.
#1369	Thomas Muir, James Cant, Thomas Baird, and William Byres, prisoners in Edinburgh Tolbooth, taken to Glasgow for shipment to America 8.3.1774.
#1371	Extract by a farmer in Kippen about to emigrate, 4.1774
#1372	In the course of last week Prince George and William and Mary sailed from Scarborough with 270 emigrants for Halifax and Fort Cumberland, Nova Scotia. One of the passengers with 13 in family constituted part of the number and it is reported he was in possession of £3,000, £800 of which he lodged in one of the York banks and took the rest with him.
	Item re a meeting of prospective emigrants from Kilsyth, Campsie, and neighborhood, 4.1774.
#1373	Item re 100 emigrants from Strathspey at Glasgow en route for New York, 4.1774.
	Adventure, Symmers, sailed from Aberdeen to the West Indies with a number of passengers 29.4.1774.
	John and Jane, Baxter, sailed from Aberdeen to St John's with emigrants 4.1774.
#1374	Christie, Craik, arrived in Antigua from Aberdeen with passengers 24.2.1774
#1375	Two Brothers, Blues, from Aberdeen to Newfoundland 13.5.1774.
#1377	Stranraer, May 5, 1774. "This morning the Gale of Whitehaven, Henderson Jefferson master, for New York, sailed from this port with 230 emigrants - 72 shipped at the Water of Fleet, the rest at Stranraer. They are mainly poor people who have little or nothing after paying their freight; a few of them are indented for 3 years having had nothing to defray the expence of their passage, nor do the greatest part of them know in what way they are to be provided for after landing."
#1381	"Wanted. Several servants to be employed in the farming way on an estate situated on the River Mississippi in the Province of West Florida - also one or two married men who would go there with their families. Enquire at Alexander Ross jr., merchant in Aberdeen. 27.6.1774."
	Item re an unnamed emigrant ship {the Bachelor of Leith}
#1383	A letter from New York

#1386   A letter from a Paisley emigrant
          Reverend Dr John Ewing, Pastor of the First Presbyterian
              Church in Philadelphia arrived in Aberdeen where he
              later preached.
          Tradesmen wanted for Jamaica ....

#1387   A letter from Charleston
          A letter from Fort William concerning emigration. Lieutenant
              John Grant, late of the 42nd Regiment, his wife and
              family, from Urquhart, Inverness-shire, together with 150
              others from Urquhart and Glen Moriston, took ship from
              Fort William to Loch Doun, Mull, where they boarded the
              Moore of Greenock, master McLarty, for New York,
              among the passengers was a James Smith, a 60 year
              old schoolmaster

#1393   Marlborough of Whitby, master Preswick, left Stromness for
              Savannah, Georgia, with 80 emigrants, 25 of whom
              were from Whitby and 55 from Orkney, 9.9.1774.

#1399   Janet and Ann, master John Youll, offered passage from
              Aberdeen to Grenada and Tobago, to sail 1.1.1775

#1400   Minerva, 300 tons, master William Gibbon, offered passage
              from Aberdeen to Grenada, and Tobago, to sail 1.1775.
          Hercules, 25 tons, 8 carriage guns, master Moses
              Cadenhead, offered passage from Aberdeen to
              Grenada, Dominica, Tobago, Barbados and Jamaica, to
              sail 1.1.1775.

#1460   Extract of a letter from New York dated 2.11.1775 to a
              gentleman in Glasgow.

#1463   "On 13 October 1775 died in Philadelphia (where he had gone
              for his health) Dr Pringle of the island of Jamaica, son of
              the late John Pringle of Haining Esq. one of the
              Senators of the College of Justice.

#1467   Extract from a letter from a gentleman in Halifax, Nova Scotia,
              to his friend in Edinburgh, 2.1.1776.

#1469   Dr John Smith, born in Scotland, settled in Charles County,
              Maryland, moved to Mississippi, returned to Norfolk,
              Virginia, and Allan Cameron, another Scot who settled
              in Virginia, prisoners of the Americans at Frederick
              Town, Maryland, 23.11.1775.

#1470   Patrick Stirling of Kippendavie, died in Jamaica 12.12.1775.
          Edinburgh, 2.4.1776. "Last Friday the 42nd (Royal Highland)
              Regiment, Lord John Murray's, were reviewed... they
              are to be on board the transports destined for America

	by the 10th instant, and the 71st Regiment (Fraser's) to be on board by the 20th instant."
#1474	Extract from a letter from on the schooner Betsy in Norfolk harbor 13.2.1776 to a gentleman in Glasgow - "a ship from Nansemond with upwards of 80 passengers, all Scots factors, is expected here (Norfolk, Virginia) on the way to Glasgow."
#1476	Edinburgh, 17.4.1776. "This day 1000 of General Fraser's new raised regiment of Highlanders were to embark at Greenock for America under the command of Sir William Erskine, Colonel of the 1st Batalion. We do not hear of the 42nd or Royal Regiment of Highlanders which embarked on Friday last."
	Montague, ... Blews, from Aberdeen to the Newfoundland fishery, 18.4.1776.
#1479	Extract of a letter from an officer of the Pacific Indiaman in Boston harbor to his friend in Edinburgh 25.3.1776.
#1480	Extract of a letter from the surgeon of the Tamar in the Savannah River, Georgia, to his friend in Glasgow, 23.3.1776.
	Extract of a letter from Captain Colvill of the Betsey which sailed from Greenock to Boston, dated 25.3.1776 Nantasket.
#1484	Extract of a letter from an officer at Halifax to his friend in Edinburgh 11.5.1776.
#1492	Extract of a letter from Quebec to a merchant in Aberdeen dated 26.6.1776, brought by Captain Smith of the London.
#1496	Anne, transport, Captain Denistoun, from the Clyde with 120 of light infantry of Fraser's Highlanders, was on 8 June taken by 3 American privateers and carried to Marblehead.
#1498	Sergeant Stirling of the 42nd Regiment, sailed from Greenock to Halifax, at Staten Island 30.7.1776.
#1506	Warwick arrived in Greenock from New York after a 31 day passage, 11.11.1776.
	York, Captain McVey, and Katy, Captain Harvie, arrived in Port Glasgow from New York, 14.11.1776.
#1516	"Wanted. Some men and women servants, mostly young, to settle in Canada and to sail for Quebec in the Spring. Every encouragement will be given. Apply to William

Brebner & Company, merchants in Aberdeen."
27.1.1777.

#1521   Nelly, McNaught, and Brunswick, Service, sailed from New York 18.1.1777 and arrived in the Clyde 2.1777.

#1522   Extract of a letter from a gentleman in New York to his friend in Edinburgh, dated 8.1.1777, re his escape from rebel hands.

#1523   General Howe, Salkeld, sailed from New York 3.2.1777 and arrived in the Clyde 3.1777.

#1523   Extract of a letter from an officer of the 42nd Regiment to a friend in Glasgow, dated 15.1.1777 in Piscataway.

#1524   Extract of a letter from gentleman in New York to a friend in Glasgow 2.2.1777.

Peggy, Gray, from Aberdeen to Newfoundland with goods 19.3.1777.

#1525   Mrs Harvey, widow of late Alexander Harvey in Antigua, died 3.1777.

#1529   "For New York. The Hercules, James Davidson master, will sail about 3 weeks hence. For passage apply to W. Brebner and Company or to the Master." 28.4.1777.

#1531   Harry Michie, late tenant in Backhill of Castle Fraser, accused of forgery, petitioned for and was granted banishment to the Plantations for 14 years, at Aberdeen 8.4.1777.

#1535   Hercules, Davidson, sailed from Aberdeen for New York 6.6.1777.

"Wanted for West Florida. A house carpenter - any such well recommended will find suitable encouragement by applying to Alexander Ross jr., merchant in Aberdeen."

Sharp, Laurie, arrived in Greenock from New York in 28 days.

The brig Crawford, late of Glasgow arrived at Whitehaven on 26.6.1777 with 110 seamen and women and children taken off different ships by American privateers. The sloop Merrin of Greenock, Neal Taylor, was sunk; the brig Jenny and Peggy of Irvine, William Howe, was sunk 20.6.1777; the brig Jenny and Sally of Glasgow, William Drummond, sailing from Glasgow to Norway was taken and sent to France, by the American privateers Reprisal, Wickes, Lexington, Johnson, and Dolphin, Nicolson, off the coast of Scotland.

#1542   Sir John Nisbet of Dean who was believed to have drowned in South Carolina was found alive and well having been driven by storm to a French West Indian island.

#1545   'We are sorry to acquaint the public that American Privateers have begun their depredations in our seas.' 8.1777. Captain James Wilson, commander of the Royal Bounty of Leith, returning from a whaling voyage to Greenland was captured by the American Privateer Tartar of Boston, John Graham, off Ronaldsay - the crew of the privateer were said to be English, Irish, Scots, Dutch, French and Swedes, including several from Orkney and Shetland.

#1546   "Wanted. A house carpenter and a mason to go to the West Indies. For particulars enquire at Provost Jopp." 8.1777.

#1547   Extract of a letter from a gentleman in Sorel to a friend in Aberdeen re military affairs.

#1548   Report of 50 Scots merchants arriving in Greenock from Virginia via New York dated 29.8.1777. Peter Wallace married Miss Harris, only daughter of Thomas Stoakes Harris in Stoakesfield, parish of St Thomas in the East, Jamaica, 12.5.1777.

#1549   "Notice. The nearest relation or heirs at law of James Cooke, a wright who lived for a good many years in the West Indian islands but died about 18 months ago, are hereby desired to apply to the printer of this newspaper and they will hear of a person who will put them in the way to obtain some money left by said James Cooke." 9.1777.

#1550   Lilly, Cochran, and York, McVey, arrived in the Clyde 9.1777 having left New York 12.8.1777.

#1551   Reference to an American ship, master McLeod, loaded with tobacco, indigo and rice, being seized at Stornaway, despite claims by the skipper that the ship was bound from the West Indies to Rotterdam.

#1552   Janet Hislop, accused of child murder, petitioned for and was granted banishment to HM Plantations for life, at Glasgow, 4.10.1777.

#1553   Dunlop arrived in the Clyde from Quebec bringing news of the war. Mary, Buchanan and Isabella, Thomson, both from Grenada; Monimia, Morrison, from St Vincent; Albion, McGregor, from St Kitts; Alexander, Bayne, Christian, Campbell, Chance, McLeran, Nancy, Thomson, Britannia, Scott, Molly, Thomson, and Friendship, Sand, from Jamaica, all arrived in Greenock with sugar and rum, 10.1777.

#1554   "Wanted. A house carpenter to go to the West Indies - good encouragement will be given. For particulars apply to John Chalmers, Westfield."

#1556   Extract of a letter from a gentleman in Canada to a friend in Aberdeen re the military affair at Bennington.

Sophia of Leith, master John Aire, was captured by the rebel privateer Black Snake of Salem, master John Coutts, 9.1777.

#1558   "For Grenada. The ship Aldie, Peter Brown, who will be clear to sail from Leith the 7 December. For passage apply to Messrs Ellis, Martin and Company in Leith. The Aldie, will call at England for convoy."

#1567   Alexander Chalmers, 48, late in Antigua, eldest son of Provost William Chalmers of Aberdeen, died in Peterhead 9.1.1778.

Extract from a letter from an officer in Philadelphia to his brother in Edinburgh, 29.11.1777.

#1569   Extract of a letter from a gentleman at Montego Bay, Jamaica, to a friend in Edinburgh dated 3.11.1777 concerning a great storm there and the wreck of vessels including the brig Boyd of Glasgow and Jenny of Glasgow, Kerr, and the drowning of most of their crews and pasengers.

Extract of a letter from Tobago to a gentleman in Aberdeen dated 20.10.1777 refering to the capture of the American privateer Black Snake.

#1570   Anne, Boyle, arrived in the Clyde from Philadelphia, 2.1778.

Three Brothers of St Thomas, Alexander McLean, was detained by the Customs in Orkney on suspicion of being American.

#1572   Extract of a letter from Dominica to Edinburgh dated 20.12.1777 relating how the 16 ton brigantine Katie fron the Clyde had been taken into government service there.

#1578   John Gordon, from South Carolina, died in Bordeaux 4.3.1778.

#1580   "We have had advice by a letter brought by a vessel from St Augustine that Charleston, South Carolina, is burnt to ashes." 4.1778.

#1581   Hercules of Aberdeen, Davidson, arrived in Aberdeen from Philadelphia. 4.1778.

Extract of a letter to Aberdeen from Philadelphia 7.2.1778.

Report from Edinburgh about the pillaging of Lord Selkirk's house in Kirkcudbright by the crew of an American privateer.

#1582   Extract of a letter from Dumfries dated 25.4.1778 concerning the American privateer Ranger, which was raiding the neighborhood. The ship's officers were named as Captain John Paul Jones, 1st Lieutenant Thomas Simpson, 2nd Lieutenant Elijah Hill, Sailing Master David Cullen and Lieutenant of Marines Sam Wallensford, and a crew of 140 men. The captain was a native of Scotland, born John Paul, late master of the John of Kirkcudbright, who had been tried for murder but had escaped.

#1584   Hercules of Aberdeen, Dunlop, from Aberdeen to Philadelphia with wine, 13.6.1778.

#1587   Sir William Erskine, McNaught, arrived in Greenock from Philadelphia, 6.1778.

#1591   Leveller of Port Glasgow, a sloop and a privateer, master William Dunlop, brought a ship into Port Glasgow which he had captured between Bordeaux and Charleston, South Carolina, 7.1778.

#1592   Betsy, Barber, and Resolution, Cox, arrived in the Clyde from the West Indies, 7.1778.

Report from Kirkwall that an American privateer was operating nearby, 20.6.1778.

#1593   Fincastle, a privateer, Stewart, brought a Congress brig Dispatch, Brown, which had left Charleston 14.5.1778, into Glasgow.

#1594   Loyal Subject of Glasgow, Andrew Sym, captured the sloop Greyhound, and took it to New York.

#1595   "Wanted for Dominica in the West Indies, a house carpenter, well qualified in that business and understanding something of machinery. Such a one properly recommended will hear of good encouragement by applying to William Forbes in Aberdeen." 8.1778.

#1600   Julian, Ledston, arrived in Aberdeen from Quebec bound for London with a cargo of furs, 7.9.1778.

#1606   William Bartlett, Assemblyman and Captain of the Royal St George Volunteers, died in Carriacou, near Grenada, 6.1778.

#1607   Eclipse of Baltimore, Jonathan Clark, a prize ship, was brought into Port Glasgow by the privateer Prince of Wales of Port Glasgow, 10.1778.

#1608   Friends of Glasgow, McFarlane, which, when returning from the Leeward Islands, had been, taken by an American privateer but later retaken by a Liverpool privateer and taken to Cork, Ireland, 10.1778.

#1610   Extract of a letter from St Johns, Newfoundland, to a gentleman in Aberdeen reporting the taking of St Pierre, 11.1778.

#1616   Elizabeth, Howe, arrived in Greenock from Halifax, Nova Scotia, 22.12.1778.

#1619   "Wanted to go to Grenada. A cartwright and a blacksmith, properly qualified in their respective trades, who will meet with good encouragement by applying to Adam Duncan, lintdresser in the Gallowgate. They must be speedy in their application as the gentleman they are to serve intends they should go out in the first fleet from London." 1.1779.

Extract of a letter from an officer on board the Unicorn, Captain Ford, at New York, 12.10.1778, regarding the taking of the American continental frigate Raleigh.

#1621   Extract of a letter from New York dated 24.12.1778.

#1622   Report that Colonel McDonnell's Corps was to embark at Kinghorn for Spithead and from there to America.

Katie, Harvie, arrived in Greenock from Halifax 2.1779.

#1627   Greenock, McLarty, from the Clyde to Jamaica 27.3.1779.

#1630   Shipping from the Clyde 27.3.1779: for Jamaica - Alexander, Bain, General Dalling, Spiers, St Andrew, Scott, Catherine, Murdoch, Christian, Bain, Hannah, Moor, Jamaica, Pollock, Westmoreland, Hunter; for Grenada - Castle Semple, McKinlay; for Tobago - Sally, McGregor; for New York - Minerva, Morrison, and Jean, Montgomerie; for Quebec - Nancy, Hunter, Juno, Orr, and Betty, McDougal; and for St Augustine - Endeavour, Spiers.

#1636   Resolution of Glasgow, Lamont, when sailing from St Kitts to Honduras was taken by an American privateer, 3.1779.

#1639   Neptune of Portsoy, James Scott, was captured off the Western Highlands by an American privateer, Independence of Boston, Brown, but later escaped, 13.5.1779.

#1641	The brigantine Hero, Morris, sailing from the Clyde to Newfoundland, liberated the Elephant, which had been captured by the privateer General Mifflin of Boston.
#1644	"Colonel Scott is appointed Governor of St Vincent and this day the Colonel passed through Edinburgh on his way to that island."
#1657	Betty and Becky of Boston, Grindal, when sailing from Boston to Amsterdam, with a cargo of tobacco and dyestuff was captured off Scallaway, Shetland, by the tender Africa, Lieutenant Hunter, 10.1779.
	"The Edinburgh Regiment, which went to America with Admiral Arbuthnott, is stationed on Long Island."
#1659	Extract of a letter from an officer of the 63rd to his friend in Edinburgh, dated Stoney Point 8.8.1779.
#1671	Tartar of Virginia, was captured off Stornaway and brought to the Forth by a Folkestone privateer, 1.1780.
#1673	Extract of a letter from Grenada, dated 23.10.1779.
#1684	"Wanted for Jamaica - a well qualified housewright who also understands the cartwright business. Likewise wanted an experienced mason, both must be of unexceptional character and well recommended. One or two young men who write a good hand and understand accounts, if well recommended, are wanted as clerks or bookkeepers on a considerable estate in a healthy situation. For particulars enquire at Alexander Abernethy, merchant in the Broadgate, Aberdeen." 17.4.1780.
#1698	Extract of a letter from Kingston, Jamaica, 3.6.1780.
#1699	Ruby, Ranken, arrived in Greenock from New York 25.7.1780.
#1711	Extract of a letter from a passenger on the Patty, Marquis, which when sailing from the Clyde to New York was attacked by an America privateer.
#1719	Hazard, arrived in Greenock from Charleston 12.12.1780.
#1721	Extract of a letter from a gentleman in St Kitts to his friend in Stirling, 22.10.1780.
#1722	Extract of a letter from an officer at Quebec to his friend in Edinburgh, 24.10.1780.
#1736	Tom Lee, an American prize ship taken by the Carleton and brought to Greenock, 4.1781.
#1739	Hero and the Mercury arrived in Greenock from New York, 5.1781.
#1750	Extract of a letter from a gentleman in Charleston, South Carolina, to his friend in Edinburgh, 1.5.1781.

#1751   Extract of a letter from a letter from a gentleman in St Lucia to his friend in Glasgow, dated 11.6.1781, giving an account of the war in the West Indies.

#1752   The brigantine Concord of Jersey, John De Feu, with wine for Quebec and Newfoundland was captured by the Robin Hood of Boston, Sergeant Smith, and sent to Boston, 22.6.1781.

#1754   Brigadier General David Ogilvie died on St Eustatia 5.1781.

#1756   Rodney, Gardner, arrived in Greenock from Georgia, 9.1781.

#1757   "Wanted for Jamaica. A cartwright, also two masons or dykers who will indent for three or four years. A little advance in money will be made for fitting out, a steerage passage from Glasgow will be paid for, and good wages, with bed board washing lodging and a surgeon to attend in case of sickness, will be allowed. Apply to Mr William Paterson, minister at Logie Buchan, or David Morice sr., advocate in Aberdeen."

#1758   "On Sunday night {10 September} arrived in Leith harbor the Gustavus the III, an American brig with a rich cargo of silks, teas, China, etc. a prize to the Lively, privateer. She was bound from Gothenburg to Philadelphia and was taken about seven leagues to the north east of Shetland." 17.9.1781.

#1759   "Advice was received yesterday {16 September 1781} from Captain Machell of the Lively privateer, fitted out from Leith by Messrs Ramsay Williamson and Company that on the 5th inst. Shetland 20 leagues North West, he captured the Beckie and Hariot, Captain Moses Grindle, an American brig from Amsterdam bound to Boston with a cargo of various merchandise and that on the 6th inst., 15 leagues north west of Shetland he captured the Four Friends, Captain William Gibbons, an American snow from Amsterdam bound to Boston with a cargo of various merchandise, one valued at £8000 and the other at £20000...."

#1760   Phoenix, Cunningham, arrived in Greenock from Newfoundland, 9.1781.

#1761   A letter from Mr Ferguson, late Governor of Tobago.
Sally, McGregor, Britannia, Buchanan, Elizabeth, Steel, Cassandra, Kinnear, Rebecca, McCall, Providence, Gardner, arrived in the Clyde from St Kitts, Friendship, Service, arrived in the Clyde from St Lucia, and

93

	Glasgow, Thomson, arrived in the Clyde from Barbados, 10.1781.
#1765	Extract of a letter from Quebec dated 21.8.1781.
	Extract of a letter from William Allen, gunner of the Allegiance, at Spanish River dated 12.8.1781 to his friend in Leith.
#1766	Extract of a letter from an officer of the 40th Regiment in New York to his friend in Aberdeen dated 20.9.1781.
#1767	Extract of a letter from an officer of the 54th regiment in New York to his friend in Edinburgh dated 6.9.1781.
#1768	Extract of a letter from an officer in New York to his friend in Edinburgh dated 18.10.1781.
#1770	Eliza of Glasgow, Captain Foster, was taken off Cape Clear by the privateer Grand Turk of Salem, 14.11.1781.
#1773	"Blacksmith wanted. A well qualified blacksmith inclining to go out to Jamaica will meet with good encouragement by applying to Francis Logie, merchant in Aberdeen." 3.12.1781.
#1775	Molly of Liverpool, Jordan, arrived in the Clyde from Jamaica 1.1782.
#1776	Mary, Martin, arrived in Greenock from New York in 29 days with a cargo of tobacco, 13.1.1782.
	Francis Colly, born in Kinnarty, parish of Peterculter, emigrated in 1770, a builder and architect, died in St John's, Antigua, 26.11.1781.
#1777	Extract of a letter from Kingston, Jamaica, dated 2.11.1781.
#1779	Extract of a letter from a gentleman, who was captured by De Graffe's fleet last autumn, to his correspondent in Aberdeen, from Charleston 29.12.1781.
#1786	Recruits wanted for HM 99th (Jamaica) Regiment, commander Robert Skene, 3.1782.
#1788	Extract of a letter from a gentleman in St Lucia to his friend in Aberdeen 17.2.1782.
#1795	Extract of a letter from a gentleman to his friend in Edinburgh, dated Charleston, South Carolina, 22.4.1782.
#1799	Bellona, Bell, arrived in Port Glasgow from Tortula, 24.6.1782.
#1805	Extract of a letter from a gentleman in Jamaica to his friend in Aberdeen, dated 18.5.1782.
	Hope, Cumming, arrived in Fairlie from the Leeward Islands 8.1782.
#1806	Extract of a letter to a gentleman in Edinburgh, dated Camp, Quarter House, South Carolina, 9.7.1782.

#1809   Quebec, Boyd, from Quebec to London with a cargo of lumber and furs, arrived at Stromness 19.8.1782 with a captive sloop Bontram of Salem, a privateer, Captain White, which had been taken on the banks of Newfoundland. Extract of a letter from a gentleman in Quebec to his friend in Edinburgh, dated 17.7.1782.

#1832   Extract of a letter from Tobago to Glasgow dated 14.11.1782 referring to a group of inhabitants of Tobago - Mr Donaldson and two children, Mr Lauchlan Campbell, Dr Drysdale, and Mr Leith with two mulatto children - who were murdered by the crew of a ship taking them to Ostend.

Thomas Fyfe, Lieutenant of the 79th Regiment, son of William Fyfe baillie of Banff, died in Kingston, Jamaica.

#1836   Duke of Leinster, arrived in Glasgow from Jamaica, 11.3.1783.

#1839   "For America. The brig Mercury, Captain George Knowles commander, now lies to at Aberdeen for Halifax in Nova Scotia, and will be clear to sail by the first of May. The vessel is copper-sheathed, is a remarkable fast sailor, and has excellent accommodation for passengers. For freight or passage apply to Sim & Robertson or the commander on board. NB House and ship carpenters, wheel and cartwrights, blacksmiths, coopers and other mechanics will doubtless find great engagement in America." 7.4.1783.

#1846   "For Halifax in Nova Scotia. The brigantine Swallow, William Robertson master, a fine new British built vessel, burthen about 160 tons, now lying at Greenock will be ready to take on board goods by the 5th June and will positively sail in that month. Such people as incline to ship goods by that vessel must have them ready to ship by the 15th June and such as incline to take passage by her must be at Greenock by the 25th. The Swallow is reckoned the fastest sailing vessel in the firth of Clyde and will be properly fitted up for the accommodation of passengers who in the course of the voyage will be allowed provisions of the best kind. For particulars apply to David Paterson in Edinburgh, Alexander Warrand in Glasgow, Morrison and Company in Greenock, and William Forsyth in Aberdeen." 5.1783.

#1849	<u>Commerce</u>, Roger, arrived in the Clyde from Bermuda, 6.1783.
#1851	"Last week 36 families, mostly tradesmen, sailed from the Clyde to Belfast, in order to embark for Philadelphia." 30.6.1783.
#1853	Extract of a letter from New York, dated 2 May 1783, from a Scottish merchant and loyalist, formerly of Virginia.
	Extract of a letter from a gentleman of character in New York, dated 26.5.1783.
#1854	<u>Hope</u>, Cumming, arrived in Port Glasgow from Antigua 15.7.1783.
	"The <u>Jean</u>, master Francis Ritchie, now lying at Greenock is ready to receive goods on board and will be clear to sail about 10 August. The <u>Jean</u> is a good vessel, copper bottomed, and a fast sailor. For freight and passage apply to James Mitchell and Company, merchants in Glasgow." 7.1783.
#1855	Extract of a letter from Charleston, South Carolina, to a gentleman in Edinburgh, dated 16.6.1783.
#1857	<u>Matty</u>, Hunter, arrived from Bermuda, and <u>Catherine</u>, Picken, arrived from New York.
	"The return of the Edinburgh Regiment, arrived at Staten Island, under Major Gordon, amounts to 351 privates."
	<u>Fly of North Carolina</u>, John Brown, arrived in Greenock from Virginia with tobacco, 4.8.1783.
	Extract of a letter from an officer in New York to his friend in Edinburgh, 16.6.1783.
	"For Halifax. The brigantine <u>Betsey</u>, British built, burden 200 tons, Robert Hyndman master, is now taking on board goods at Greenock and will positively sail by the 5th September. For freight or passage apply to Mr John Ewen in Aberdeen, Alexander Warrand in Glasgow, or Morrison and Company in Greenock. The <u>Betsey</u> is well fitted up for, passengers and the best of provisions will be laid on for the voyage. N.B. Able bodied laborers, joiners, millwrights, house carpenters, blacksmiths, coopers, bricklayers, masons and ship carpenters who wish to go to Halifax and cannot advance the freight on embarkation will be accommodated in a passage by the <u>Betsy</u> on their engaging to pay their freight six days after their arrival at Halifax. As tradesmen and laborers are much wanted in Nova

Scotia on their arrival there they will meet with great encouragement." 8.1783.

#1865   "For Kingston and the North Side and the West End of Jamaica, the ship Mary, James Noble master, [formerly the Governor Dalling]. She is now ready to take on board goods at Port Glasgow and will be clear to sail the first week of November. For freight and passage apply to Robert Drummond and Company, merchants in Glasgow, or Patrick Dougall, merchant in Port Glasgow. A cabin passage is 20 guineas, a steerage passage 9 guineas, all stores found. The Mary is a very fine ship, about 400 tons burden and has good accommodation for passengers." 6.10.1783.

#1868   "For New York and Philadelphia. The Mary, John Heartwell master, now lying at Port Glasgow ready to receive goods on board and will be ready to clear to sail about 10th of November. The Mary is an exceedingly good vessel, double decked, and a fast sailor, also has excellent accommodation for passengers. For freight and passage apply to James Mitchell and Company, merchants in Glasgow." 10.1783.

#1870   Extract of a letter from a gentleman in Maryland to his friend in Edinburgh.

#1871   Polly, transport, Wharton, has arrived in Greenock from Newfoundland with 2 additional companies of the 71st Regiment on board, commanded by Captain John McDonald.

#1872   "Wanted immediately for the Island of Grenada. A house carpenter and wright. Any such, well recommended, will find suitable encouragement by applying to Alexander Ross jr., merchant in Aberdeen." 11.1783.

"The President and Professors of the College of New Jersey in America have conferred the degree of Doctor of Divinity on the Reverend Mr Charles Nisbet, minister at Montrose." 11.1783.

#1876   "For Halifax in Nova Scotia the brigantine Ceres, 200 ton burden, James Davidson master, now lying in the harbor of Aberdeen, will be particularly adapted for the reception of passengers; she is now ready to take in goods and freight and will be clear to sail the 1st March next. For freight or passage apply to Brebner and

Company or to the master in Aberdeen. The Ceres is a British built vessel, 3 years old, with an experienced master." 22.12.1783.

.

www.ingramcontent.com/pod-product-compliance
Lightning Source LLC
Chambersburg PA
CBHW071138280326
41935CB00010B/1279